THE COMMON GOOD CORPORATION

THE COMMON GOOD CORPORATION

The Experiment has Worked!

Robert Fishman
and
Barbara Fishman

The Journey to Oz Press
Philadelphia, PA

Published by The Journey to Oz Press

A division of Resources for Human Development, Inc.

4700 Wissahickon Avenue, Suite 126, Philadelphia, PA 19144

Library of Congress Cataloging-in-Publication Data

ISBN 0-9796324-0-4

Made In China.

Cover photographs by Ken Kauffman.

CONTENTS

COMMENTS ON THIS BOOK

It is rare to be able to create an organization that from the beginning is based upon ideals. We had that opportunity in 1970 when the Commonwealth of Pennsylvania enacted and funded its first comprehensive Mental Health/Mental Retardation Act. I was asked to form a citizen's committee to administer the program in Lower Merion Township of Montgomery County. The committee incorporated Resources for Human Development, Inc. (RHD), a non-profit corporation. Prior to receipt of our first grant of $50,000 we interviewed several candidates and hired Bob Fishman as our first executive director, and as it turned out our only executive director.

We were all caught up in the spirit of the "sixties" including the feeling that we were empowered to do anything we dreamed to make a better world. Based upon our past experiences we considered what worked and what did not work, what we enjoyed doing and what we did not enjoy doing, and what values we wanted to promote. We supported originality, imagination, creativity, the empowerment of people and ideas. We visualized the organization as a catalyst to empower people for social change. We were not bound to traditional corporate models.

This book is the story of RHD's struggle over 37 years to exist, to grow, to support its values, to question, to experiment with change even as it accomplished its phenomenal growth. How does an organization build into its structure a mechanism for renewal? How does a rapidly growing organization prevent itself from becoming the victim of rigid rules and regulations?

Bob Fishman, our executive director and co-author of this book with his wife Barbara, has been the guiding light in RHD's success story. His ability to inspire and empower people, to raise new issues and values, to resolve conflict, to anticipate the need for change, to broaden our directions, and to keep the staff, clients and funders excited, is remarkable. His work and the work of RHD has helped and changed many lives including my own. Our community and the many people RHD has touched have all been beneficiaries of this experiment.

As we, within RHD, continue our struggle questioning how we can pass on RHD's unique culture and its values to the next generation of leadership, I hope that you the reader will be inspired by this book to question your own organization and to witness that dreams can come true.

--Bertram Wolfson, RHD Board Chairperson (1970-present)

This book describes a socio-economic experiment rare in the history of organizations. There are few if any companies, public or private, that adhere scrupulously to values of respect, cooperation, diversity, equality, openness, fairness, and anti-authoritarianism while growing an average of 27% a year for 37 years! There are few if any non-profit agencies in which 3000 employees spread across 11 states manage city, county, state and federal contracts on an overhead of 15% or less, year after year after year.

If you have ever believed that nature dictates a contradiction between personal satisfaction, the common good, and economic success you will find this book an eye-opener. "We were determined at the start," writes Bob Fishman, "to demonstrate that an organization operating under the assumption of equal human worth would also prosper financially." What makes this assumption more remarkable is that RHD was founded on a principle unheard of in the world of non-profit philanthropy: that the corporation be economically self-sufficient without any fund-raising from or by its board. As an RHD board member for more than three decades and a consultant to global corporations since 1969 I have never seen anything as consistently effective both financially and socially as the values-based organization Bob Fishman and his staff have evolved.

Moreover, as co-director of one small unit, I can attest that what you are about to read relative to autonomy, trust, responsibility, dedication to service, quality and commitment goes well beyond the rhetoric of typical corporate mission statements. For 15 years Sandra Janoff and I have had unconditional support from RHD's staff and board for every decision our unit has made. No second-guessing. No unasked for advice. No snooping or policing from the central office. For our end of the bargain, we seek to live by the values elaborated here; and, by hook or by crook, we pay our own way.

Whether your issue is fiscal responsibility, compensation, leadership, decision-making, decentralization, control, social entrepreneurship, employee development, or racism, sexism and drugs in the workplace, you will find here principles, guidelines, and examples of a radical business philosophy in action. I for one find it inspiring to be part of this experiment in managing for the common good. I hope you too will be inspired to experiment with your own variations.

--Marvin Weisbord, author of Discovering Common Ground, and Productive Workplaces Revisited; Co-Director, Future Search Network.

Hal Taussig, entrepreneur, philanthropist, and recipient of Newman's Own/George Award as "the most generous business in America" observes that this book "...can serve as a model for employers who aspire to move toward more justice in the workplace."

ACKNOWLEDGEMENTS

In 1970 a group of concerned citizens interviewed me as part of their effort to launch a local mental health center that was supported by a $50,000 grant from Montgomery County, a suburb adjacent to the city of Philadelphia, Pennsylvania. That interview was significant in my life, not only because I was offered, and accepted, the job but also because the position allowed me to initiate an experiment.

I was interested in seeing whether a values-driven corporation that pursued many diverse paths could, at the same time, be financially viable. The group agreed to try this experiment. They became the Board of RHD, with Bertram Wolfson, Esq. as its chairman. While Board membership has changed over the years, Bert has remained. RHD would not be the expanding $162,000,000 Common Good Corporation it is today were it not for his vision, his belief in our experiment, and his trust in me.

Other Board members provided the support that made this journey possible. I am particularly thankful to Sheldon Steinberg, Anthony J. Parroto, Frederick Bonaparte, Edward Robinson, Avrene Brandt, Barbara Shoulson-Kuhn, Jo Ann E. Connelly, Caryn Reichlin Johnson, Marvin Weisbord, Samantha Jones-Thomas, Virginia Kricun and Cody Anderson. These members are very important to the future of this effort. I trust they will continue to demonstrate their belief in what we have begun.

Many more staff participated in the experiment than I can ever list. They include over three thousand colleagues that keep the RHD system alive today, and the many thousands that stayed with us for a while and decided to move on. Their effort has become part of who we are. I especially thank Peggy Mowatt, our Chief Operating Officer, who is an anchor and a partner. Her commitment and understanding of how to maintain a balance between values and money, has made our work possible. I also thank Sharon Kauffman, Marsha O'Hara, Michael Dennome, Dennis Roberts, Richelle Gunter, Todd Silverstein, and until recently, Mary Loomis, for helping us to blossom into the corporation we are today. Together we have spearheaded the RHD experiment.

RHD doesn't exist in a vacuum. There were and are numerous professionals in governmental offices and financial institutions that have cast their vote of confidence along the way. I continue to experience that vote from Estelle Richman in Pennsylvania. I also credit the many others throughout the country who have trusted us to care for human beings who might be disabled or emotionally injured, but who all need respectful loving attention.

I also want to express my gratitude to our consumers and the communities of people we have touched. They are what we are here for.

Our experiment would never have taken flight without the active participation of the Central Office Assistant Directors, Budget Managers, the Access Team, Unit Directors and the staffs that directly provide the services RHD is known for. I offer many thanks to the Central Office fiscal managers and their staffs, our grant writers, the information technology staff, RHD's human resources group, and the people who pay attention to insurance, property, and legal issues.

My wife, Barbara, and I wrote this book together, in the process sharing thoughts, trading drafts, and seeking the language to communicate the importance of this common good experiment. Barbara wrote from her experience as founder and coordinator of RHD's Access Team. The attention, capacity and perseverance that she brought to this book have been a crucial element in making it possible. And, she was able to lead me through a patient writing effort that doesn't fit my style.

Lastly I thank friends and family who listened to my ideas and dreams, and provided their understanding and support. My children and their families are central to that list. Others, who have helped with the writing process, include Peggy Mowatt, Michael Dennome, Alison Armstrong, and Gene Schneyer.

The RHD experiment began when we opened the doors of our original storefront mental health clinic. From that first day, I did my best to create a workplace in which trust and laughter, creativity and joy abounded. It was a place that I wanted to work in. More often than not people in RHD have actively created it with me. I hope that this writing and our website will seed these practices in many other workplaces.

Bob Fishman
Philadelphia, March 2007

BOB FISHMAN

Listening to my parents quarrel, and trying to understand why they repeatedly fought, absorbed many a night. This effort and its implications have shaped my thinking and my professional work for the past fifty years.

My parents' arguments always followed the same format: My mother insisted that she was right and that my father was wrong – and the bad one. When their fight reached a certain pitch, my father, a man of few words, angrily stomped out of the apartment, repeatedly demonstrating that he could leave her – and me.

By the time I was eleven, I figured out that neither she nor he was right – or bad. I couldn't side with either one. Later, my attention shifted to how my friends argued, and I realized that their complaints were also mostly trivial. It was the way they fought that was the problem. Without even knowing it, I began to practice peacemaking. The role required that I communicate a vision that allowed both parties to be "right." Looking back I see that this was another step in what would become a life-long effort to understand human relationships and find a better way to manage conflict.

My life took many turns in my college years as I developed friendships, found lovers, and ultimately found and married Barbara. In her I found a partner. She, too, was studying her parents' marriage. She, too, was trying to remain true to herself while connecting with others. Our marriage was going to be an experiment.

None of my teachers in college and graduate school seemed to have a vision of a healthy human relationship. They certainly taught me about relationships, but mostly I found myself studying hostile connections and the variety of ways people tried to find safety in the midst of the wars they created. Most people didn't see any way out. Why? I wondered.

The philosophers I studied produced grand, general theories but didn't plunge into the human details. Freud did, but with a pessimism that didn't match my view of life. I could never find a systemic approach to avoiding the failures.

By this time, I, too, was in the fray. In my marriage I saw how easy it was to get caught in right and wrong. What was right for me could be very different from what was right for Barbara. Neither winning nor losing seemed to work. It was confusing.

At work I was exposed to supervisors who believed that their approaches to work problems were absolutely right. They had no doubt. And in order to make their favored solutions happen they acted like tyrants. It made no sense.

Slowly, some answers emerged. I knew I needed to love and be loved – as do we all – and I knew I wanted to lead others in the search for better ways to work together.

I experimented with the radical proposition that there was nothing that could be called absolutely "right" or "wrong" in human relationships. However, I did believe it was wrong to deny others the freedom to pursue what was right for them. It became clear that people in conflict had to resist the tendency to control others and instead respect the multiple perspectives at play -- while searching for values-based resolutions. This radical proposition affirmed that ours is a world of infinite possibility. I am still excited by this proposition because it suggests that opportunities for human creativity and the common good are boundless.

RHD was conceived and developed as an experiment. Thirty-six years later, I'm clear that the experiment is about creating healthy workplace communities. The experiment confirms that large faceless groups cannot manage conflict successfully, but small working groups can – if employees are given the freedom to do so. I have come to believe that if human beings want to, they can settle almost every disagreement, but only in one time and in one place. That is what it is like to live in a world of infinite possibility.

Add to this a set of values-based guidelines that small groups can use to manage their conflicts and we are well on the road to a common good corporate effort, with all the energy and creativity that such an effort releases.

The RHD experiment has also taught me the importance of a values-driven approach to corporate fiscal management. I didn't know at the time RHD was founded just how big a part the creative and imaginative use of money would play in the common good corporate story, but so it has.

I hope that this book will encourage those of you who are RHD leaders to continue the good work that has made us successful, and that those of you readers who are in the leadership of other corporations will start or expand your own values-based workplace experiments. Economic success is an astonishing side effect. And I also ask you to join me and others at www.commongoodcorporation.com as we develop this new corporate form. There are many people in our corporate world who are searching for a values-based way to do business. Together, we can have an impact.

BARBARA FISHMAN

Having tested our capacity to be partners in raising three sons (who with their wives are now parents of our six grandchildren), Bob and I decided that it was time to take another leap – into the difficulties and joys of a writing partnership that just might produce a useful manuscript.

For at least ten years before that decision, this book has lived in my mind as a book waiting to happen. In one sense, it's the story of thousands of employees who are doing the corporation's good work each and every day. In another, it's the story of a remarkable Board of Directors and devoted corporate managers and line staff who have, over the years, shaped RHD into a common good effort.

The book is also the story of the many years that Bob and I have spent thinking about people and the workplaces they create. As parents, psychotherapists, and corporate administrators we have grown to appreciate the many-sided, and ultimately unknowable, complexity of corporate life. Accepting this essential reality, we have learned how to work with uncertainty – with information that holds only for a limited time and space.

We bring different skills to the writing of this book. Bob's thirty-seven years of experience as the CEO of Resources for Human Development, Inc. (RHD) is immensely valuable, as is his capacity to conceptualize and lead this large human endeavor in congruence with values that function as interpersonal guidelines. My twenty-five years of experience as an administrator of RHD's Access Team, which has been devoted to providing organizational development for the corporation and clinical expertise for the employees, including a counseling service, training, and education, has equipped me with an intimate knowledge of the RHD experiment.

My goal is to illuminate and thereby make these guidelines accessible to future leaders of RHD as well as to leaders of other corporations. I also want to describe a few of the hundreds of smaller experiments in common good living that Bob has stimulated within the larger experiment that is RHD.

My experience in authoring two previous books, one on healthy couple relationships and the other about the Buddhist approach to wellbeing, has taught me how to write about complexity directly and, I hope, simply.

The major components of our approach to corporate life are best viewed from a number of different perspectives – as though you, the reader, are being guided around a lake teeming with life and each view of the lake offers new information. We look at how RHD uses the same common good values to manage people, manage power, and manage money. By presenting multiple perspectives on the use of values, we develop a kaleidoscopic view of a common good corporation. No view is sufficient unto itself while the composite necessarily leaves much out.

RHD, in all its richness, is the manifestation of this kaleidoscope of views.

CHAPTER I

THE EXPERIMENT HAS WORKED.

D are we Americans believe that large corporations can nurture the human spirit? This question, in various forms, has arisen regularly both in and out of the business community over the last several decades, enduring through a range of economic, regulatory, and political climates, and through various managerial fashions. Given current evidence of corporate greed and abuse, the question is even more urgent. Is it at all reasonable to hope that corporations can imbue organizational life with a noble purpose – the pursuit of the common good? And if a corporation commits itself to the common good, can it achieve financial success with a return to investors?

Business's reaction to these questions runs the gamut. Many corporations either ignore or outrightly reject the idea of values-based operations; they do so in the name of maximizing shareholder return in the short-term, regardless of the effect on other stakeholders such as employees and local communities. Other corporations rhetorically embrace the concept, issuing statements about corporate citizenship, financial transparency, and social responsibility, but accompany their PR with scant or token efforts. Happily, still others, including such notables as Ben & Jerry's Ice Cream and Stoneyfield Yogurt, strive to embrace the effort, and find their commitment amply repaid in high employee morale and healthy market share.[1] The leaders of such corporations are pioneers

---

[1]Cohen, Ben and Warwick, Mal. *Values-Driven Business*. San Francisco. Berrett-Koehler Publishers, Inc. 2006

who courageously instituted a range of values-based operations.

Resources for Human Development, Inc. (RHD), the company at the center of this book, falls decidedly into the category of businesses that devote themselves to common-good ideals. Having started in 1970 with a $50,000 contract to provide community mental health services in suburban Philadelphia, RHD is now a national, diversified non-profit business providing more than $162 million worth of services across eleven states and the District of Columbia each year. It is comprised of an ever-growing number of service delivery systems, which we call units. Our ventures include but are not limited to community living opportunities for people who are mentally ill, developmentally disabled, drug and alcohol addicted, criminally adjudicated, and homeless. We also operate outpatient mental health centers, serve troubled children in their homes and schools, and provide rehabilitation and new construction of low- and moderate-income homes. In our affiliated for-profit effort we oversee $19 million in venture funds and have equity positions in a number of businesses.

RHD was conceived as an experiment in values-led entrepreneurialism, and has been run that way through all its existence. Just about everything we have done has been consciously grounded in a specific set of common good values. These values are expressed in how we hire, fire, assign benefits, plan our finances, handle money, distribute power, make decisions, and more. We infuse our values into leadership, marketing, production, and the distribution of profit.

In pursuing these values, our staff has generated a surging revenue stream, with a growth rate averaging 28% per year during our thirty-seven years of existence (two of those years at 150-200% and most years at 15-25%). We are living, prospering proof that when all stakeholders are linked by common-good values, the potential for financial success and sustainability is incalculable.

Our answer to whether corporations can nurture the human spirit is a resounding yes.

> RHD was conceived as an experiment in values-led entrepreneurialism

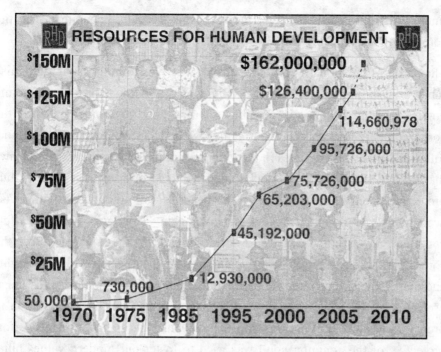

RESOURCES FOR HUMAN DEVELOPMENT

$150M — $162,000,000
$125M — $126,400,000
$100M — 114,660,978
95,726,000
$75M — 75,726,000
65,203,000
$50M — 45,192,000
$25M
12,930,000
730,000
50,000
1970 1975 1985 1995 2000 2005 2010

While conducting the ongoing RHD experiment, leaders and staff have learned how to develop workplace communities, support local decision-making, and institute unique monetary policies. We have consciously steered away from authoritarian styles of leadership, and operated on trust unless proven wrong. We have attended to the economic and social needs of all "stakeholder–owners" including managers, line staff, consumers, the corporation itself, as well as the communities affected by the corporation. In fact, we identify RHD so strongly with the values-led path that we now refer to ourselves as a "common good corporation."

In some ways this paradigm is not new; the American corporation was in existence in the original thirteen colonies. If the project was in the public interest, entrepreneurs could request and receive a corporate charter from the state. That charter could be revoked if the project proved to be injurious to citizens of the community. During the entire colonial period, however, only about a half-dozen business corporations were chartered; between the end of the Revolution and 1795 this rose to about 150. It was only after the Civil War, when economic conditions favored large enterprises, the national grid of railroads was being constructed, and investors needed vast amounts of capital (more than the partnership form of business could generate), that the corporation was actively used.[2]

The power of the modern corporate business derives from its capacity to raise funds from unlimited numbers of people, thus generating enormous economic power. Looking back, it is possible to track how government shaped the corporation for that entrepreneurial need. In 1856, for instance, England, followed by the United States in the latter half of the 19th century, passed laws that limited the liability of stockholders to the worth of their shares, thus protecting them from the risk of tremendous loss that would otherwise accompany the potential for tremendous gain. This governmental effort continued in America when, toward the end of the 19th century, the corporation was deemed to be a free and independent person with legal rights and duties. Intriguingly, the rights to "due process under the law" and "equal protection of the law" were originally incorporated into the Constitution to protect freed slaves. What was originally a values-based governmental effort protective of the common good was used to foster our modern values-blind economic endeavors.[3]

There was, however, still one more impediment to corporate growth – the governmental oversight that was written into early corporate charters and was still in place. During the early years of the twentieth century state governments jettisoned those restrictions from their corporate laws. And now, with the powerhouse that is capitalism in full force, and the very notion of oversight forgotten, the modern corporate form has become a dominant business behemoth.[4]

That corporate behemoth is certainly well entrenched at the beginning of the 21st century, but like all human social creations, it is subject to change. And recently it has become obvious that removing state mandated obligations from powerful money-making engines have come with serious negative social and environmental consequences. The time is ripe for a re-examination of the behemoth we have created. Listen closely and you can hear the groundswell of

[2] Sam Smith. *Shadows of Hope*. Indiana University Press. 1944.
[3] Joel Baken. *The Corporation*. Viking Canada. 2004.
[4] Ibid.

objection across the world. It falls upon this generation of business people to join that groundswell and address the lack of values-based corporate behavior. And in so doing reshape the corporation for socially responsible ends.[5]

In light of this important business thrust, the common good corporation, RHD being our prime example, creates value and wealth – by embracing and promoting employee and community wellbeing. How do we do this? It all starts with the three basic assumptions that underlie our values-driven and practical approach to human and corporate behavior – assumptions that are put into practice.

THREE BASIC ASSUMPTIONS OF THE COMMON GOOD CORPORATION

Is it possible to measure the worth of a single human being? The Declaration of Independence doesn't even consider the question meaningful. It assumes that human worth is a given, that everyone has it in equal amounts: *"We hold these truths to be self-evident, that all men are created equal."*

People, that is, are of equal human worth. And, as our Constitution makes concrete, this applies across the breadth of our nation, and across the wide differences in our population. Our first assumption, its roots deep in American history, expresses this basic truth.

Assumption Number One: People Are Of Equal Human Worth.

That no person is more inherently deserving than any other may be easy to accept in the abstract, but putting it into a business context, and putting it into action, results in a profound departure from the way most corporations do business. As RHD sees it, this first assumption indicates that we must continuously question whether what we do – large, small, corporate-wide or local – allows all stakeholders to experience themselves as of equal worth to one another. This results in a number of practices, from teaching employees from very different cultures and backgrounds to work together respectfully, to

---

[5] Ibid.

eliminating status markers of the type that executives elsewhere take for granted, to striving to equalize the distribution of money. Much more will be said on this and the other assumptions later in the book, but for now, suffice it to say that as great as is our commitment to this principle in our daily work lives, the benefits we reap in return are greater still. A corporation is not a machine, but rather the coordinated effort of human beings. Allowing these human beings to experience themselves as equal in human worth makes it more likely that they will be highly productive corporate citizens, whether in a boardroom or a working group.

Many business leaders, unfortunately, conflate human worth with market value. It would be commonplace, within the walls of an ordinary American corporation, to hear someone say, "Joe is worth every dollar of the $200,000 we pay him." In reality, however, Joe's market worth has nothing to do with his human worth – and to assume that the two concepts are one and the same makes it all too easy to slip into treating workers or consumers as commodities, expendable items in a cost-benefit analysis.

A classic example is the Ford Motor Company's reputed approach to a defect in its Pinto cars and trucks during the 1970's. These vehicles had gas tanks that ruptured during low-speed rear-end collisions, spilling gasoline and risking fire. It has been reported that some executives of Ford did a cost-benefit analysis that indicated that fixing the cars would cost more than settling projected insurance claims. In this accounting, Ford attached a price to each human life – an actuarial calculation – added to that number legal fees, potential insurance claims, and so on. As it turned out, recalling and fixing all of the cars would cost more than the "market value" of the human beings affected (i.e., the cost of paying off claims brought against Ford for their injuries and deaths). Because they considered human worth and human market value to be one, they didn't take human worth into account, and declined to fix the cars. Ultimately 500 people burned to death in crashes.[6]

The second assumption is difficult for many to accept in the corporate context, because businesses are often based on the belief that people aren't essentially good, that they cannot be trusted, and that leads to the assumption that

---

[6] Mark Dowie. *Pinto Madness*. Mother Jones Magazine. September/October 1977 issue

authority is needed to keep workers trustworthy. With this distrust comes a large investment, financial and otherwise, in risk control. Regardless, the truth of the second assumption – and the evidence of its contribution to success – grows out of thirty-six years of data from RHD. It is that people are essentially good, unless proven otherwise. And therefore so are all corporate stakeholders, employees as well as managers.

Assumption Number Two: People Are Essentially Good, Unless Proven Otherwise.

It was Will Rogers who said, "I've traveled this world long enough and have met so many good people that I'm having a harder and harder time believing that people are basically bad." This has been RHD's experience.

The assumption that people are essentially good unless proven otherwise allows us to trust our employees. Many corporations would assume that operating under this principle would leave us open to all manner of theft, abuse, and missteps. In practice, however, our theft and abuse rate is certainly no higher than it would have been without trust, and probably lower. Our many trustworthy employees – that is, 99 out of 100 – are treated with the dignity they deserve, and they respond with loyalty and dedication; the very few untrustworthy employees very quickly show themselves, are dealt with, and we move on.

The assumption that people are essentially good also allows us to build trusting relationships with the governments that buy our services. Indeed, we see ourselves as colleagues in the effort to produce the best service we can. Given this honest and open relationship, governments come to us for help. They sense the trust we have in them and reward us with trust of their own.

On another level, the assumption of the essential goodness of employees allows us to delegate responsibility in a multiplicity of matters usually reserved for management. We trust employees with the care of their consumers, with information, marketing decisions, contract decisions, and the management of money. We believe, and have seen our belief borne out again and again, that conditions of trust not only allow employees to live up to expectations and thrive as individuals, but also, as employees, to innovate, take initiative, and take "ownership" of their work in ways that contribute greatly to RHD's success.

...the assumption of the essential goodness of employees allows us to delegate responsibility in a multiplicity of matters usually reserved for management.

The first and second assumptions emphasize a respect for and openness to others. The third has to do with openness, too, but in this case, it is openness to ideas and to new solutions. Just as other people – other employees – have worth, and just as management has no exclusive claim on personal value or goodness, other ways of doing things besides typical business practice conceived by management, are worthy of consideration. Since there is not one right way to run a corporation or solve corporate problems, openness to new thinking, and to ideas from other people, is essential. In fact, it results in innovation – sometimes from unlikely sources (much more on this later in the book). Our final assumption, then, that there is no single way to manage complex corporate issues, is a fitting third in this trio of trust in people, intentions, and ideas.

> Both/and thinking refers to the effort to find solutions that balance multiple interests.

Assumption Number Three: There Is No Single Way To Manage Corporate Issues Well.

Because our world is endlessly changing, we can only know it contingently, as a probability. Corporate leaders and staff members are challenged to understand the corporation itself as a probability. Its present form is the result of many variables that fell into place. And we cannot absolutely know, but rather only predict that the next corporate development opportunity will fall into place. True, it might *feel* like a sure thing, but that's very limited information. All forecasts must stand the test of reality.

Paradoxically, this assumption presents corporate personnel, be they staff or managers, with the challenge of taking risks – even as they are aware that they cannot *know* the best course to take. This means acting on their best educated guesses. And because each action is based on a guess, leaders cannot be blamed for guesses that prove to be wrong. Gathering the courage to act, they let others know of the limited knowledge upon which a decision is made, and then move forward. In a sense, every action is a "draft." RHD is an organization in the process of continually and consciously creating drafts.

Another practical expression of the assumption that there is no single way of managing corporate issues well is what we at RHD call "both/and thinking." This is the opposite of either/or thinking. Both/and thinking refers to the effort to find solutions that balance multiple interests.

The Basic Assumptions
of
the Common Good Corporation

- People are of equal human worth.
- People are essentially good.
- There is no single way to manage
  corporate issues well.

Rejecting unnecessary dichotomies – both/and thinking – opens up a large space between the poles of two competing or opposing interests, a space that offers room to look around, to consider various options, and possibly to find the formulas that, at least partially, satisfy all.

Both/and thinking allows a corporation to tackle issues that appear insurmountable. What is a seemingly insurmountable business issue often is a result of defining the problem as a dichotomy. Without both/and thinking, for instance, the debate between short-term financial benefits or long-term sustainability can harden into fixed polar positions that offer no room for compromise. The addition of both/and thinking to this debate, when tied to a search for the common good, produces more thoughtful, nuanced alternatives that allow for a range of potentially workable outcomes, even if the ideas aren't quick, simple, or totally satisfying to any one group.

The three basic assumptions, recall, are supported by RHD's bottom line. They enhance financial success through a range of very practical applications as we manage people, money, and power. The assumptions echo through everything we do, from the briefest employee-to-employee interaction to the longest term, farthest-reaching corporate decision.

The following chapters will explore the ways in which our basic assumptions inform our larger corporate and financial structure. They will detail how a common good corporation really works – how our values shape our day-to-day operations. They will tell the story, too, of what it means and how it feels to be a common good stakeholder, an experience that in our case has some unusual intensity, as RHD's primary field – human services – is one in which emotions are often raw and decisions can be life-or-death. First, we'll take a broad look at how our principles guide us in the management of people, power and money, thus creatively releasing the vast amount of productive energy for corporate work.

CHAPTER II

THE COMMON GOOD CORPORATION
MANAGING PEOPLE, POWER AND MONEY

"The freedom started from the first day we were hired. Like most RHD employees, we weren't given job descriptions; instead, many of our job responsibilities were self-assigned and self-monitored. There were very few 'oughts' or 'shoulds.' It was simply expected, though not necessarily stated, that we would do something constructive on behalf of others. And if we could be creative as well, it was never discouraged. In fact, it was celebrated. None of us take this for granted. At the drop of a hat we can tell the painful stories of friends who work in very different circumstances."

–Dennis

All corporations, whether non-profit or for-profit, large or small, need people: their labor, their commitment, and their creativity – their "people energy." The greater and more widespread the people energy, the better the corporation's results will be, and the more likely it will be to succeed. The question then becomes: How is that energy created, focused, and released?

Our American founders had an answer: to include citizens from all walks of life into the process of making decisions about the governance of our country. Jeffersonian democracy, recall, was consciously designed to call forth participation: to give citizens a say in how government was elected into power, spent money, what laws were passed, and how taxation was managed. From thirty-six years of experience we at RHD know they were right. In the tradition of this wisdom, stakeholders of all sorts are engaged in current corporate issues. We promote opportunity, encourage and respect diversity of opinion, and do what it takes to ensure everyone has a voice. And we hold fast to the understanding that continual debate and ongoing change will always be necessary. In this sense, RHD is a supremely American corporation.

Surely there are many ways to translate democracy into corporate life, but the RHD experiment has proven that the common-good, values-led approach does the job. And it works spectacularly well. Taking this approach means that, as guided by the three basic assumptions introduced in the last chapter, we treat people as having equal human worth, we assume they are good, and we assume they can add value to decision-making (as there's no one way to manage corporate issues well). This management approach creates employees who are engaged in their work, customers who participate in the design of the product they intend to buy, funders or investors who actively promote a project, rather than discouraging it or passively maintaining their neutrality. This is the kind of vital corporate energy – people energy – that produces success.

Like any corporation, we manage people, power and money, but we do so in search of this energy. And we add a unique twist. In each of these categories, we focus more on community than self-interest, we rely more on cooperation than competition, and we move away from elitism to the kind of egalitarianism valued so highly by the founders of our country. Of great importance, this values-based effort affects all stakeholders – from the Board to top management, supervisors, line staff, financial people, the customers we serve, and the government agencies who contract for our work.

PEOPLE

As a common good corporation, RHD's management practices include, among others, the creation of small workgroup communities, rules of behavior that foster equal worth, the use of space to increase communication within and across workgroups. This produces workgroups that pull together and support a colleague when one of them does well.

Creating Small Workgroup Communities

This is at the heart of RHD's management of people. While most large corporations, IBM, GE, etc., encourage workers to identify with the corporation as a whole, we encourage people to identify with their small workgroups. Experience teaches us that a workgroup community is more likely to emerge when there are face-to face relationships that develop in groups of up to forty people. First, a worker identifies with this community and only then with the larger corporation.

> The more a corporation adheres to the equal
> worth assumption, the more it becomes
> a common good corporation.

The more a corporation adheres to the equal worth assumption, the more it becomes a common good corporation.

When a workgroup is at its best, people feel it's *their* community; they *belong* to it. And their actions show it. If a member is sick, it's very likely he or she will receive concerned telephone messages and get-well cards. Birthdays, engagements, marriages and baby showers are celebrated; pictures of vacation experiences are shared. At RHD's central office snapshots of people who attend Christmas parties, employee baseball games, or Martin Luther King Day celebrations cover the walls. And the same is true at many unit offices around the corporation.

We know that certain rules of behavior are necessary for these workgroup communities to flourish. And as you will read in the next chapter, our values are formulated as guidelines or practical rules for use in these workgroups. These rules foster the respect, trust, multi-level thinking and the both/and thinking that sustains communities particularly during hard times when it's the local group that has to pull together to solve a problem.

We are continually looking for ways to build community. In that effort, small groups are very creative – they develop retreats at the beach or in the mountains, community art projects, sports teams, etc. In the Central Office we have found that food is an excellent community builder. So we often serve food at meetings – it's a way to attract people who avoid "dry" topics such as "Understanding Your Unit's Budget." And there's always food in the lunchroom – leftovers from a meeting or the remains of someone's weekend party. It's not rare for employees to say that RHD feels like an extension of their family. As an expression of that feeling, employees have created a special fund called Heart-To-Heart, which offers help to someone in serious trouble due to illness or accidents.

"If you're sick or in trouble, RHD is a good place to work. When Joan was undergoing surgery, radiation and chemotherapy for cancer, she was able to come into work when she felt she could function and stay home when that was impossible. And when my mother moved toward death, many people expressed their concern. When she died, the church was filled with RHD people. I'll never forget that."

–Cecilia

Encouraging The Positive Status Conferred by Groups On A Member.

This is particularly important when that group member functions well or leads effectively. We also maximize the status of the person who contributes to the *productivity* of that workgroup. Individuals who try to gain status in *competition* with others lose status in our system.

At the same time, we minimize the status bestowed by leaders from the top down. We are aware that typical corporations use positive status as a reward, which only managers can bestow, and they do that sparingly to boost competition among the few individuals who manage the organization. To counter this practice, in RHD we challenge any leader who provides special status to individuals they prefer. Instead, we consistently support the status conferred by a workgroup on productive members.

"Small groups," we often say, "make us happen." I recall sitting in a meeting of one of those small groups – the Values Committee. Six people were talking about a videotape they had just created. They were excited about the creativity and the humor they brought to their acting. Wrapping up at the end, the leaders applauded the performers and the performers applauded the leaders, in so doing

"Small groups," we often say, "make us happen."

14

offering each other status. And the status for the entire group grew as the videotape was shown across the corporation.

Because these small groups are so important to our success, we employ facilitators who specialize in enhancing their work. Leaders or managers who seek to improve a group's process can request that a facilitator work in on-going meetings or create a retreat.

Using Space As A Management Tool

Unlike traditional corporations where space is used to recognize the few – top management and individual leaders – at the expense of the many, we use space to further an egalitarian approach to people. For instance, we have no separate lunchroom for managers. Everyone, including consumers, eats together. There are no personal parking spaces. We have no private offices; the director of the homeless shelter works side by side with staff members. Our Central Office front-desk staff, in fact, has become accustomed to the bewilderment of first-time visitors. When people come to see the CEO – me – they often ask for the executive suite. "Really," the receptionists insist, "there is no executive suite. He sits right over there by the window. And when he wants private meeting space, he signs up for it like everyone else." And I've grown used to the visitors' well-meant, but unnecessary commiseration. "How can you do without the quiet? The privacy? I could never work that way!" "Ah," I nod. "Spend a moment looking around. Watch people approach each other about a work problem. Watch them make decisions together. Listen to what they say."

What the visitors see and hear is a working environment in which everyone has access to everyone else, information flows freely, and decisions can easily be made in consultation with others. They see workers who, symbolically as well as substantively, are respected as much as managers or anyone else in the corporation, who know they are valued and that their creativity is desired; and who thus are highly engaged. They see employees who understand that others in the office have something to contribute, and who are therefore open to different ways of solving problems, different ways of pursuing opportunities. That, to me, and to the other members of RHD management, defines our workplace community, and counts for infinitely more than the glories of the executive office space.

> [This] is a working environment in which everyone has access to everyone else, information flows freely, and decisions can easily be made in consultation with others.

Very few of our managers leave us for more conventional workplaces because they miss the status, the space or other perks that usually come with such positions. Most are motivated by the deeper satisfaction that comes with collegiality, achievement, and cooperation, and the pride they feel working in a supportive, nurturing workplace. Whether for-profit or non-profit, these workplace characteristics address basic human needs. It feels good to live a values-based life, to work in a community, in small groups that validate our equal human worth, to recognize that we all have something of value to offer.

> *"As a new Unit Director I've gotten a lot of encouragement from the Central Office. Over and over again my managers tell me to create my vision. They trust me. And that has given me the opportunity to put my own imprint on my program. No one told me how to do it. This freedom makes it possible for me to offer my staff what I would have appreciated when I was doing direct service."*
>
> *–Ray*

POWER

A common good corporation spreads power as broadly as it can. RHD's goal is to increase the power of all employees, and to give as many people as possible a creative or critical voice. We do this by attending to how people in the corporation use their power as they relate to each other, and by creating a corporate structure that, in itself, distributes power.

In a common good corporation, power is managed so as to increase the participation of employees who are not owners or key managers in setting corporate policy. The more employees feel empowered, the more the corporation is able to achieve common-good objectives.

Using Power Well Is A Skill

Knowing no other way to lead, managers in every other corporation I have known misused their power. And employees became their victims. In order to use power well, a manager must, first and foremost, be aware of its presence.

In a common good corporation, power is managed so as to increase the participation of employees who are not owners or key managers in setting corporate policy. The more employees feel empowered, the more the corporation is able to achieve common-good objectives.

Only then can he or she use it respectfully. Ask most corporate managers or administrators whether staff is frightened of them and you're likely to hear some rendition of "No one needs to be afraid of me" or, "I'm a fair and considerate person." While that might be true, it doesn't negate the fact that any leader, good or bad, has the power to deprive someone of a salary. That power alone provokes fear. Ask any corporate employee and you'll hear stories of fiefdoms, tyrants, and fear – right in the middle of our modern business world.

In search of the common good managers in RHD openly acknowledge the existence of power – most importantly, their power to fire an employee. Accepting the responsibility that goes with this recognition is a major challenge. To manage this power well in RHD, we distribute it locally, to unit directors and their staffs. And we ask that hiring and firing decisions include the concurrence of the director and at least one other person – it cannot be based on the whim or even the considered opinion of one individual.

As you will see in the next chapter, our values provide the same guidelines regarding the management of power for all employees. In a workgroup each person has power. That power can contribute to, or diminish, the functioning of the workgroup. There is no successful workgroup I have ever seen that avoids conflict; instead, a successful workgroup demands a skillful use of power. RHD's values teach how to manage conflict and exercise power without diminishing or degrading others. This teaching has to be an ongoing effort of any common good corporation.

Decentralizing Power Wherever You Can

Remember, our principles tell us that people are essentially good, which means they can participate in making corporate decisions. It is no coincidence that this is exactly what the founders of our country believed, or that, like them – and like most others who believe in American democracy – we find leadership in the manner of kings and queens repugnant.

This approach to power was illustrated for me several years ago when RHD was selected to replace another provider that had been managing a large homeless shelter for men. Given the angry staff currently working at the shelter, the disrepair of the facility and the high visibility of the effort, it was a major RHD challenge. I recall sitting around a table with several line staff from the shelter, two Central Office fiscal people and the Unit Directors. In effect, it was an impromptu, pick-up meeting. No one had been appointed to the effort but everyone was interested in the challenge. I watched as one line staff member said that there wasn't ever enough food to go round in the shelter, and the new Unit Director suggested that the group literally make food to celebrate the change in management. A financial person added that we ask government to increase the food budget. The brainstorm continued around the table with creative contributions cascading, one after another. This energy continued for several months in regular meetings. Power came with participation.

The company is organized into small, semi-autonomous, decentralized units to spread power. Units provide a context for employees of different rank to work together in small face-to-face groups to shape their workplace, find their mission, and to generate quality products.

Individual unit directors hold the right to contract with local vendors, to establish unit-specific approaches to care, and, if they have demonstrated the requisite skill and judgment, to enter into direct negotiation with governmental authorities for new business. Whether the topic is the layout of new office space or the hiring of a new employee, it is accepted practice that the unit makes the decision – with as broad a consensus as possible. Leaders cannot assume that positions they favor will be blindly followed – even as CEO, my positions certainly aren't. In short, RHD, as a common good corporation, empowers a wide range of people to get the job done well. In so doing, we communicate our assumption of trust to more than 3,200 employees. Not an easy task.

> *"When I learned that RHD would give me the room to be more creative in my work, it got my attention. After all those years in a bureaucracy, I wanted that creativity badly. Right now we're readying a house for two new residents. After I learned that one of them collects old spoons as a hobby, I went out and found a bunch of old spoons in a used furniture store. This morning I arranged them in a collage on one of the walls. This afternoon I'm going to another used-furniture store to find some other interesting items for the house. It's part of how we have the freedom to recognize the personal interests of the people who live with*

*us. The houses aren't stamped out; they're individualized, designed. And
the effort is within budget. We're all really excited."*

–Dale

That is the stakeholder-energy every corporation searches for. Feeling trusted,
being empowered, staff members thrive. Many other stakeholders thrive as well,
including our consumers and the governmental departments that contract with us.

Since we are functioning in the American business culture, certain corporate
powers must be centralized. RHD needs to relate to the banking system,
demonstrating our fiscal integrity by centralizing fiscal data from across the
entire system and preparing auditable financial records. The Central Office also
has a system of checks and balances for programmatic oversight, and a
contracting system that assures government of our capacity to deliver services.
And we provide legal oversight and insurance that protects the entire system. Put
all these services together and you have a powerful centralized corporate
machine that has managed over $1.3 billion in funding over the years without
audit exceptions.

However, there is a problem inherent in the system. This centralized corporate
machine includes personnel who must use centralized power to get their job
done, and if unchecked, this use of power can spread across the entire
corporation. To counter this possibility, or rather likelihood, as you will see in
Chapter V, we have created policies and structures that move toward
decentralizing power.

Upcoming chapters will detail the uses, implementation, and implications of
decentralization and centralization, but no overview of how our values affect
productivity can omit the profound impact on creativity, the morale super-
charge, and the energy produced by trusting our employees with power.

> Since we are
> functioning in
> the American
> business culture,
> certain corporate
> powers must be
> centralized.

MONEY

Money, of course, plays a critical role in the way the common good corporation
lives its values with regard to stakeholders. It is consciously used to reward,
motivate, or cultivate the many rather than the select few. It is used to create

community rather than to reward hierarchy. Chapters VIII, IX & X are devoted exclusively to the differences between the typical and the common-good, values-driven approach to fiscal matters – and the profound implications of those differences.

In a common good corporation, money is managed so as to address the needs of the corporation's stakeholders, including managers and employees, as well as the communities that the corporation affects. The more a corporation addresses the fiscal needs of its employees and communities in this search for balance, the more it is a common good corporation.

There are very specific ways in which the common-good management of money affects the well-being of all stakeholders. It will probably not come as a surprise that RHD does not centralize fiscal decision-making among managers whose private offices are high up in large corporate buildings. Nor do we pay high salaries for managers and leaders. Instead, we use money to create the conditions that foster community, and encourage personal expression and creativity in workgroups. Money, among all the other things it can do, represents another aspect of corporate life that RHD uses to develop, focus and release stakeholder energy.

We also draw a distinction between "operational" and "discretionary" money. Not unlike other businesses, operational money is that which is spent on operational expenses – ongoing costs at the level of last year's operations, cost-of-living increases for corporate employees, and the current costs for overhead (borrowing, rent, and the like). Unlike many other businesses, however, local groups manage operational money.

Placing Trust In Managers And Employees To Handle Operational Money

In essence, we delegate many fiscal decisions to local units. We can do this because of our second basic assumption – that stakeholders are good unless proven otherwise, and because of our third basic assumption – that there is no one way to manage corporate issues well. We have proven to ourselves that our trust in the value of multiple perspectives works, and we know we gain by doing so. Our approach empowers as many as possible to innovate, make decisions, and take action with money, thus generating stakeholder energy.

> In a common good corporation, money is managed so as to address the needs of the corporation's stakeholders, including managers and employees, as well as the communities that the corporation affects. The more a corporation addresses the fiscal needs of its employees and communities in this search for balance, the more it is a common good corporation.

This financial aspect of the decentralization of power (discussed earlier in this chapter) means in practice that we use a unit-based budget system. This allows for responsible spending close to the point of service. Almost all purchasing decisions, for example, are done at the unit level. They are guided by unit budgets, and reviewed by central office budget managers. In RHD residential programs, for example, local employees furnish living spaces, outfit offices, and buy food as well as household supplies for, and when possible, with consumers. In some cases, the cost of those locally-bought purchases runs somewhat higher than it would have if the buying had been centralized, but our corporate gain far outweighs the loss of economies of scale.

Not everyone, however, is trustworthy or fiscally competent. Sometimes people use operational money poorly and their budgets show shortfall. Sometimes we have to take a unit's financial freedom away – but we give the unit an opportunity to re-train themselves; indeed we provide mentoring. Sometimes we need to hire a new Unit Director or the unit needs to hire new staff members. But when the unit is ready, it tries again. Our experience is that failure due to fiscal misunderstanding is rare. And failure due to dishonesty is extremely rare.

More common is local employee success and the pride that comes with it. The unit is much like a small business. Management and staff see it as their own creation – so much so that employees are sometimes motivated to promote RHD's organizational model to outside organizations.

> *"I was sitting with a group of occupational therapists, discussing our work, when Julia described how difficult it was to get the supplies she needed in another organization. She talked about requisition forms that went through several layers of corporate bureaucracy and took several weeks to find their way through the system. I told her that in RHD our group had a budget, and that we could spend down for supplies whenever we needed them – immediately, if necessary. I also suggested that she speak to the managers of her corporation about creating a budget for her group. I even offered to do it with her, and bring some examples of our budgets with me."*
>
> *–Stacy*

We have proven to ourselves that our trust in the value of multiple perspectives works...

One example of our values-driven use of operational money – and one of the important ways we create stakeholder energy – is to be as fair as we can in regard to salaries. Our "maximum multiple" policy establishes a maximum ratio between my total compensation as the CEO and those who receive the lowest compensation. This policy also applies to other executives, which means that more money is available for common good purposes.

Pursuing Common Good Goals With Discretionary Money

This is money that remains after operational expenses are met. Discretionary money offers a common good corporation a way of striking a balance amongst the needs of all our stakeholders, including the corporation itself, top managers, employees, and the communities we affect. More on this in chapter IX.

How a corporation uses its discretionary funds, and whether those funds are used to enrich top management or address employee and community needs, reflects the organization's underlying values. Our values at RHD lead us to distribute most of our discretionary funds among workers in the form of bonuses and extra benefits such as training and education, scholarships, employee assistance programs, and insurance. We provide a wide range of in-house training and education opportunities, as well as a scholarship fund for those wanting to pursue formal education. Our Employee Assistance Program offers ten free counseling sessions for employees and/or their families during every year of employment. And the corporation provides short-term disability insurance and subsidizes a credit union. Each year – a small thing that means a lot – we sponsor a summer corporate picnic for workers and their families along with other events.

A major way we use our discretionary funds according to our values – and in so doing generate stakeholder energy – is our policy about raises. Unless we are making a specific effort to boost the lowest salaries, salary increases, when they can be given, are distributed equally within working groups.

In 2004, for example, everyone in the corporate office was given a three percent raise. This benefited the higher-wage employees more than the lower-wage employees, as, obviously, three percent of a higher salary is more money than three percent of a lower one. To help flatten that tilt, therefore, we also gave each employee a salary boost of $400.00. The lower the salary, the more that amount affected the percentage of wage increase. The combination of percentage increases and the fixed amount resulted in the lower-wage workers netting larger raises relative to their incomes than the higher-wage workers. Not only did everyone know that was our aim, but the extra money made a real difference to our lower-wage workers. Mary, a single mom with two children and a salary of $26,000, told me, "That $400 check will pay my dental bill – and I'll have enough money to pay for a day at the beach with my kids."

> *"Sometimes, at the end of each budgetary year, if my unit has discretionary money available, we give everyone a flat bonus. Because it's flat, our lower paid people get more than they would if the amount was based on a percentage calculation. After all, 10% of my salary would absorb a much larger amount of that discretionary money than the salary of a line worker. When Debra, a line worker, got her $1000, she whooped for joy "Now I can pay my car repair bill."*
>
> *–John*

Also central to our discretionary fund policy is that everyone has equal ownership in our benefit system. This means that new employees are fully vested in our retirement fund, and each worker has the same percentage of salary applied to a benefit package. In most corporations, of course, the financial contribution of those who leave during the first few years (usually the lowest paid group) isn't returned to them, but instead remains in the benefit pool; this benefits those who stay for longer periods, primarily management. By contrast, in our fully vested retirement fund, long-term employees do not benefit from a high turnover rate, and those who leave take their retirement dollars with them.

The kind of employee interest and loyalty this generates was demonstrated just last week. As I walked down a hall in the office, a woman stopped me, asking, "You're Bob Fishman, aren't you?" It turned out her name was Amanda, and she remembered me from a speech I gave in 1988. "I worked for RHD's Head Start program," she said, "and I was also a Head Start mom. I've just graduated from college with a major in business. Now that I'm looking for a job, I decided to visit because I remember your talking about the values, and how RHD tries to be fair to lower-paid employees, and that even the benefits are more fair than in other corporations." It's no coincidence that in following our values in these and other ways of handling discretionary money, we generate considerable stakeholder energy.

As you will find throughout this book, our common-good values, in this case in relation to money, actually spur a kind of upward spiral of ever-increasing benefit. Because we operate on the principle that our employees have equal human worth, we set our fiscal policy – both operational and discretionary – so as to personally benefit employees in a way that promotes equality, and in a way that empowers them. This increases our employees' morale, loyalty, creativity, and motivation, which in turn improve our services. Which generates more income – to distribute according to common-good values.

What we see in RHD is the marvel of people pulling together, experiencing community and feeling empowered. Again and again, we find examples in which the extraordinary is accomplished because employees are given the trust and the means to do so.

RICK

This is a story about one of those "Friday-at-five" calls. The kind that come in when you're ready for the weekend – in this case, July 4th weekend – half out the door, and more than half tempted just to let that phone ring.

The call was from a government administrator at wit's end. There was not a single bed available in Connecticut's entire Department of Mental Retardation system, he said, and no one was able to move any mountains before a holiday weekend. He had no idea what to do with a man who had just come into his charge, Rick, who was forty-five, developmentally disabled, in a panic, and without anyone to care for him after the unexpected death of his father. He was waiting in the Emergency Room of the hospital where his father had been having routine surgery. Could RHD-Connecticut do anything, anything at all, to help?

No immediate solution presented itself to Paul, the Director of RHD-Connecticut. He was pretty sure, actually, that RHD's beds were full, just as the Department's were. Regardless of the uncertainty, however, regardless of the holiday, regardless of the time, Paul didn't hesitate. "Yes, of course, we will help." He wasn't a top executive, but he knew that as a Unit Director at RHD he had the power, as well as the responsibility, to make something happen.

That evening Paul contacted Bill, one of RHD- Connecticut's Behavior Specialists, who also had plans for the weekend, but was more than willing to be interrupted. As Paul and Bill talked, they recalled that the two of them had worked with Rick several years before in a day program created by another provider. "Both of us knew that Rick could become violent and actually hit people or break things," Paul recalls. "As we looked further into his medical records, we read that he had a dual diagnosis" – he was both developmentally disabled and mentally ill – "and he had an obsession with the music of Barry Manilow. Rick's father would be driven to distraction after hearing a Manilow song twenty or thirty times." If asked to stop, however, Rick would pick up a glass or a jar and throw it. "It was clear that Rick would certainly be a challenge," Paul remembers, "but I thought the staff and the other residents could meet that challenge, especially if they were prepared."

Within a few hours after the phone call from government, Paul had mobilized a team based at Sunset House, one of our family-like homes. He didn't have to ask for permission from the Central Office to mobilize the team, he simply knew it was needed and acted.

The Sunset House team offers round-the-clock staff to serve four developmentally disabled people. On that Friday, Mary, the Sunset House nurse, called Rick's doctors and found a way to transfer his medication prescriptions to Sunset House – no easy task. Tracey, the House Manager, led the Sunset House team in moving quickly to dismantle the site's office and make it into a bedroom. The office was small, too small for the long term: for now it would do. Again, no central permission was necessary, only the need, the knowledge, and the employees empowered to help someone in urgent need.

The residents were gathering that evening for a group event so Cassandra, RHD-Connecticut's Assistant Director, took the opportunity to tell them about Rick and his sadness at the death of his father. Cassandra and the residents talked about offering Rick a temporary home in what was the office, and that perhaps someday they could give him a permanent home at Sunset House, if they could renovate the garage. Not everyone was happy about the idea, but one resident after another agreed that it was important to help Rick out. After all this took place, Paul phoned his supervisor, not for authorization, rather for suggestions.

On the very same Friday that Paul got the initial call, Rick made the transition from the hospital to Sunset House. A staff member picked him up at the hospital and when Rick opened the front door, the residents gave him a big welcome. Paul remembers, "Rick grinned as he recognized me, took in all the smiling faces all around him, and cheerfully proclaimed, 'This is my new home.'"

"Sometimes," Paul recalls, "you know when you have done a good thing. And that day we did a *really* good thing."

The vital interplay of RHD's values and delegation results in the success that is perfectly illustrated in Rick's story. Our first basic assumption, that all people have equal human worth, guided us in offering Rick a respectful and caring response to his desperate need. Our second basic assumption, that people are good unless proven otherwise, allowed our local Unit Director to work with government to solve a problem quickly and without a contract, with the expectation and the trust that we would get paid for it (we did). And our third basic assumption, that there is no single way to handle corporate issues well, gave us the flexibility we needed for everything we did. If we had tried to solve Rick's problem from the central office, we would not have had enough information either about Rick or the local unit, to make wise decisions, or to avoid delays while we got up to speed; delays or missteps would have caused further misery to Rick and inconveniences to our governmental customer. Also the local staff group would have felt imposed upon, which is not a productive way to get a job done. Clearly, an RHD group with a face-to-face relationship with our governmental customers and with our consumers was a practical way to find a solution to Rick's problem, and was empowering for all.

RHD employees are not any different than the employees of other corporations; empowerment hasn't made people perfect. They make their mistakes, as you will see later in this book. What we aspire to do, and what we continue to achieve, however, is to manage status, power and money, according to our basic assumptions – and that has made us highly generative of stakeholder energy. It has made us a profitable and sustainable common good corporation.

As I often say to stakeholders, we have a tiger by the tail.

CHAPTER III

VALUES-BASED WORKPLACE BEHAVIOR

As we discussed before, every corporation develops a particular personality, a culture of its own – and values, whether consciously or unconsciously chosen, are always embedded in that culture. These values show themselves in many ways; among them, the behavior of leaders, the design of corporate offices, the type and quality of products produced, and the way employees relate to each other. This suggests that the choice of values and the examination of their implications is very important work – if leadership does not decide which values to promote, a corporation may unconsciously adopt some of the worst that the broader American culture offers.

In this chapter we'll look at common good values and how they affect the way employees relate to each other. Applying the values to employee interactions is a very conscious endeavor at RHD; indeed, we ask all working groups to discuss and demonstrate an understanding of these values. For this reason, new employees do well when they purposely observe how seasoned employees relate to each other, and if confused, ask one of them to explain what's going on. Those who assume that because they have worked elsewhere they know how to conduct themselves will likely make all sorts of mistakes.

The values, which, remember, grow out of our three basic assumptions (that people are of equal human worth, that they are essentially good unless proven otherwise, and that there is no single way to run a corporation well) stimulate significant creativity, commitment, and entrepreneurialism. And the RHD experiment proves that they harness stakeholder energy to fuel success.

From the employee's point of view, the values are interpersonal guidelines. As such, the Values Group realized, they don't offer enough information for a workplace that is very complex. And so we began to tease out the how-to-do-it instructions built into each value.

Then we presented them on videotape, in classes, and in written form, making it more likely they would be debated and taught. If an administrator had to manage a disagreement he or she could take a course or read about how to express his or her point of view clearly, powerfully and respectfully. And if a line worker felt unfairly treated, he or she could watch a videotape or read about how to deal with conflict clearly, powerfully, and respectfully.

Shortly I'll share the nuts and bolts of common-good workplace behavior – and the process by which common-good behaviors were identified. But first I'll take a step back so you can understand how I came to use a values-based approach to corporate behavior.

The seeds of this approach to human relations were sown within me when I was a child – soon after World War II, the Holocaust, and the bombings of Hiroshima and Nagasaki. I was about twelve when I read about the ghastliness of the violence, and the horror burst inside me with the power of one of those bombs. Searching for some way to deal with what I was reading – and my reactions to it – I began to pay attention to Gandhi's work in India and to the American Quakers' rejection of war. When the time came to register for the draft, I applied for, and was awarded, conscientious objector status. Later, I was drawn to Martin Luther King and the Civil Rights Movement.

Whether or not you lean toward my particular approach to violence, every one of us has to deal with the human conflict that emerges in corporate life. We do well when we manage that conflict consciously and so minimize the short-lived skirmishes that might develop into long-term feuds. Everyone suffers when such conflicts are not properly managed.

After working in corporations for several years I began to understand that business as usual, given its authoritarian structure, was another, if less lethal, expression of violence. That expression of violence is possible when those at the top of the organization are assumed to be inherently "worth more" than those lower down, and the former are justified in imposing their desires and decisions on their subordinates, and are welcome to disregard the subordinates' concerns or welfare, except to the extent that it serves the executives' own desired ends.

With this insight, my vision of a career took shape: I would create a workplace, and perhaps an entire organization, that was both guided by the assumption that people are of equal human worth *and* attentive to the bottom line.

Happily, this dream struck a chord with the community leaders who first interviewed me for the executive director position of the yet-to-be-born RHD. By that time, I had already played a major role in developing the Pennsylvania Hospital's Community Mental Health Center and its community-based health system – a leap in the development of services within Philadelphia. When they became aware of all this experience, my interviewers naturally asked why I wanted to start again with a completely new and relatively small enterprise. But when I began talking about the abuse of employees I had witnessed within corporate environments, they quickly understood my motivation. Indeed, they began sharing their own disturbing corporate stories. Those experiences led them to the same conclusion – it was time to try something different. Soon we were talking about experimenting with a safer, more people-friendly business environment – one that we would later call a common-good approach to corporate life.

Much to my delight, this group of community leaders ultimately decided to empower me to launch the RHD experiment. Together, we were determined to demonstrate that an organization operating under the assumption of equal human worth would also prosper financially.

As soon as our storefront mental health clinic opened, the employees and I began to examine our values, write them down and translate them into the behaviors we would follow. And I began to realize the ramifications of these values for me in corporate life. It struck me that even though I was the founder, the "boss" of this corporation, adhering to these values meant I wouldn't be able to impose a corporate directive – even when I was sure it was the right thing to do. This was a huge challenge. It still is.

...adhering to these values meant I wouldn't be able to impose a corporate directive – even when I was sure it was the right thing to do. This was a huge challenge. It still is.

Nevertheless I worked with my fellow employees to clarify the behaviors we wanted to accept and those we wanted to reject. We were a small group joined together to shape our behavior. I came to understand that because we knew each other in a personal way – in a face-to-face workgroup – we were more likely to implement and maintain these values. So I knew that to create an entire values-driven corporation, there would have to be many such small workgroups or communities. Only in this format could the meaning of the equal human worth assumption be felt, discussed and re-discussed, and the recommended behaviors followed.

I find it easiest to understand the meaning behind this assumption when I think of my children. I feel deeply that as human beings they are all of equal worth, and I have no interest in measuring or comparing their human value. I have somewhat less emotion tied to assuming the equal worth of all the people who work in RHD, and it's harder still for me to feel this toward people in other countries with whom I have no contact. Distance and large numbers weaken the emotional power of this assumption of equality. And when an assumption stops being heartfelt, it becomes nothing more than an abstract idea. It loses its punch. Therefore, small workgroups are essential to my vision.

For a few years our values meetings were an informal effort that included, as they do now, both management and line workers. Over time the process became more formal: we teased out the behaviors we wanted to promote, wrote them down, distributed them to everyone, discussed the suggested changes, and then adopted them. I believe this is a very important job for a corporate executive or anyone striving to develop a common good corporation. I still do it. And it takes time.

The result of this effort was the RHD Values Statement (and subsequently, the RHD Bill of Rights, about which more presently). It's an agenda for behavior at work, a condensed version of which is displayed in every meeting room. By no means are these statements empty words. At meetings, when people talk about incidents that have occurred or decisions to be made, heads reflexively turn toward the statement on the wall; participants are identifying which values are relevant to the discussion. And then they go on to discuss how the value applies to the issue at hand.

The Values Statement has always been considered a draft; people know that it is in continual development. In our ongoing Values Group we review and consider revising the current document. The values are also celebrated at a yearly Values Day Celebration attended by many of our staff and consumers. This tradition now occurs at several locations around the country.

When an employee talks about working in "the RHD way," he or she is affirming that this values-based thinking is part of the culture. The comment is also evidence that our corporate values serve a cohesive culture-building function. Management helps this along by expecting every employee will attempt to walk the values path – whether they're in agreement with the values or not. Not every RHD employee is able to do so; indeed, some choose to leave the organization. But they are a small group.

In my experience, employees feel safer, more grounded and sure of themselves because they share these values.

> The Values Statement has always been considered a draft; people know it is in continual development.

RHD'S VALUES STATEMENT

Respect For The Dignity And Worth Of Each Individual: Employees and consumers have the right to live and/or work in an environment that affirms their fundamental dignity as human beings. This is an important guideline for line staff as they work together and with consumers. It is also important for managers as they supervise staff members.

Multi-level Thinking: RHD promotes a "win-win" thinking process that encourages the expression of many different viewpoints and rejects one-dimensional thinking. This value, actually a skill that can be taught, increases an employee's capacity to deal with varying viewpoints. Given the diversity of our workforce and our assumption that there is no *one* right way to run a corporation, multi-level thinking is necessary.

Empowerment of Groups: At RHD, power resides within small groups, not with the individual. Group leaders are empowered to empower others; but no person, regardless of position, has permission to treat others in an inappropriate or dictatorial manner.

Decentralization of Authority: Local decision-making should be maximized and, whenever possible, power and responsibility should not be centralized but instead reside in the small working group. Given our belief that employees are essentially good unless proven otherwise, we trust that they will use their authority well.

Safe and Open Environment: All RHD settings must be open environments where employees and consumers feel safe to communicate their thoughts, feelings, and concerns without fear of ridicule or retaliation.

Creativity: All consumers and employees should be actively encouraged and supported to express fresh ideas and approaches, regardless of the degree to which these ideas depart from what is typical or commonplace. RHD's safe and open small group environments foster creativity. And because creativity is essential to corporate success, employees are encouraged to express their ideas regardless of how far those ideas depart from the norm.

Honesty and Trust: All RHD environments are expected to be places of honest communication, which promote and support the belief that each consumer and employee is worthy of trust, and will always be treated with respect.

Diversity: Diversity with regards to characteristics such as race, age, gender, ethnicity, culture and level of education, economic status, religion, and sexual orientation is valued and promoted by the organization as a rich asset. The corporation rejects all discriminatory behaviors toward any individual or group and thrives on debates that derive from human variation.

Organizational Integrity: RHD embraces the obligation to conduct all of its work with strict adherence to the highest ethical standards. The ends do not justify the means.

Ongoing Growth and Development: RHD is committed to constant improvement and the growth that fuels its capacity to address new social issues.

Personal and Professional Enrichment: RHD is committed to creating environments that promote the maximum enrichment of the personal and professional life of each consumer and employee.

Quality Service: All programs are required to deliver quality service that assesses consumer needs and satisfaction, evaluates service outcomes, and is the result of an ongoing process of teamwork and group participation.

Every one of these values is grounded in our three basic assumptions. The first assumption – people are of equal human worth – is the basis of our respect for the dignity and worth of each individual. The second assumption – people are essentially good – leads to the many small groups that are empowered to make RHD happen. And the third assumption – there are many ways to manage a corporation well – leads to the decentralization of authority. No value can be interpreted in a way that is in contradiction to the basic assumptions. The complete version of RHD's values is in Appendix A.

From these values we have identified specific interpersonal guidelines employees can use in their work lives. They have been assembled in a document called *The RHD Bill of Rights and Responsibilities*. It serves as the framework we strive to live by, describing concrete ways that employees can act, consciously and with forethought, so as to create a common good corporate culture. We strongly encourage each employee to read and think about the *Bill*, and to participate actively in making the RHD environment in which he or she works reflect the *Bill's* spirit and intent *The RHD Bill of Rights and Responsibilities* appears in its entirety in Appendix B. We also encourage the reader who works in, or is leading, another corporation to advocate for, and develop such a document then please share the experience with us on our web site: www.commongoodcorporation.org

The following examples offer a sampling from the Bill of Rights that are basic to the RHD culture.

A Safe and Open Environment

Basic to RHD's corporate culture, and therefore basic to the *Bill*, is the belief that employees and consumers have a right to live and work in an atmosphere that respects the dignity and worth of each individual. In order to make this belief a reality, it is important for workers to create a safe and open workplace, one that encourages the expression of diverse ideas and viewpoints, accepts conflict and the appropriate expression of anger, rejects hostile behaviors, and strives to operate by consensus rather than through centralized authority.

One reason to be explicit about our values and our behavioral norms is that we, like many other corporations in our country, are very diverse in color, ethnic background, sexual orientation, and modes of thinking. So we need vehicles for managing, supporting, and at times, transcending, this diversity. This isn't easy. For many individuals, diversity creates a fear of the unknown, a fear that can emerge as conflict and confusion. For others it is a joy and a source of ongoing creativity.

The reality of diversity at RHD is that employees working side-by-side might hold, for example, very different sexual orientations – one might be homophobic and the other homosexual – or very different attitudes about authority – one might be obsequious, the other rebellious. RHD's values serve all these employees because diversity itself is honored, and the skills needed to work with diversity are taught.

Non-Hostile Expressions of Anger

The entire values effort, as I explained above, began with a focus on managing discord well. No surprise, then, that staff members and I, working together on the values effort, realized that employees had to learn how to manage conflict if RHD was to become a common good corporation. We all had to develop the skills necessary to be angry without becoming hostile, and so avoid falling into destructive behaviors. Yes: employees at RHD are consciously educated about how to disagree civilly and they are held to that standard.

...it is important for workers to create a safe and open workplace, one that encourages the expression of diverse ideas and viewpoints, accepts conflict and the appropriate expression of anger, rejects hostile behaviors, and strives to operate by consensus rather than through centralized authority.

The section of the Bill that deals with anger begins this way:

> Anger, or the surge of emotion that comes with strong differences, is a normal part of conflict in the workplace. Even though we may be upset as strong feelings are expressed, we must avoid being hostile with one another. Those that fear the expression of anger are likely to suppress their feelings and not share their ideas. This in turn slows and reduces the effectiveness of the overall corporation.

In this work environment, everyone has the right to have his or her own viewpoint on any topic. When a viewpoint is different or in opposition to that of others, it's important not to discount it. Instead, RHD develops in its staff members the skills necessary to deal effectively with difference.

Those skills include:

- Being clear about your feelings and thoughts
- Confronting the right person – or the true source of your anger – not others
- Using "I" messages to own your feelings and thoughts and to decrease the defensiveness of the other person(s)
- Including others in a discussion rather than speaking only for your self

While conflict and anger are acceptable at RHD, hostility is not. We ask common good employees to identify hostile behavior and to reject it. Probably the simplest hostile behavior to identify is addressed as follows:

Intimidation or explosion in behaviors such as yelling, inappropriate language, or physical threats are clearly destructive to interpersonal safety and are not acceptable at RHD. The culture itself holds the message that this hostility "is not the way we do things." When it happens, as it occasionally does, this message gives people – managers and line staff of small workgroups – a standard to act from, whether that is to simply indicate that the hostile person has gone too far or to suggest a conflict management course. Needless to say, not everyone can learn how to manage their anger well, and it is those people that we hope will stay at RHD for only a short time.

Demeaning speech is another example of hostile behavior. It includes name-calling, ridicule, sarcasm, or anything else that undermines a person's self-esteem and implies he or she is less than worthy as a human being. It is clearly unacceptable at RHD. If a leader tolerates a member of the group – whether staff member or client – being ridiculed, that leader is allowing for hostility. Anyone encountering such hostile behavior has the responsibility to surface it as an issue.

The way this gets put into action at RHD is well illustrated by a conflict that occurred between an African-American fiscal assistant, Jamile, and his Hispanic colleague, Juan. Just this year during a Property Department meeting Jamile used ethnically based sarcasm as a put-down to Juan. Juan, however, was savvy enough to recall a values discussion in which participants talked about avoiding humor that hurts. He remembered that the first article in the Bill of Rights and Responsibilities *advocated the avoidance of humor that was disdainful of groups, regardless of race, ethnicity, or sexual orientation. As Juan spoke about this, others joined with him; they, too, knew about the value and its importance.*

The group debated the use of such humor, and, with the help of their leader, came to a decision: to ask Jamile to reconsider his use of sarcasm. Jamile agreed, and promised not to make such remarks in the future. He wanted the group acceptance and he wanted his job. Meanwhile, his fellow employees were protecting their department's safe and open environment.

The threat of abandonment in the work environment takes the form of either the employer's implied threat of dismissal or the worker's implied or direct threat to leave. Such indirect or subtle threats are sometimes used as a weapon. Threats of firings or resignations create the desire to withdraw from relationships, reduce creative risk-taking, and undermine the feeling of safety.

When such events arise, it is important that communication about job performance be clear and open. Supervisors need to be explicit regarding the reasons for possible termination; employees deserve to know that their jobs are secure unless they are clearly warned to the contrary. Similarly, supervisors need to know if an employee is planning to leave so that strategies can be designed to cause the least amount of disruption to co-workers.

Carrying negative triangulated messages is another hostile behavior that is discouraged at RHD. Triangulated messages are angry comments (supposedly or actually) made by someone not present, which are then repeated; namely, when A tells B that C made a negative comment about B behind B's back. When that happens we say that A is acting as a carrier of a negative message to person B.

If a staff member hears such a triangulated message, we suggest that he or she (A) avoid becoming a part of the triangulated pattern, and instead, encourage the person who made the comment (C) to speak directly to the person who is being criticized (B).

Here's an example: Jane, an RHD employee, placed a small radio on her desk. She played it softly, but not softly enough for Sean, who sat next to her. Sean told Alicia about his problem with Jane. Alicia, without Sean's knowledge, told Jane that Sean was angry with her, that he had called her selfish, and had said that the radio was much too loud. Hearing this, Jane got angry with Sean and stopped talking to him. Sean realized something was wrong but couldn't figure it out.

Several weeks later, Jane attended an RHD class on conflict management, and heard about the importance of speaking directly when involved in a conflict, and the problems that occur when people triangulate. Realizing that this is what had happened to her, Jane asked Sean if he was bothered by her radio. His face flushed; he admitted that the radio was indeed interfering with his concentration on numbers. He, in turn, asked Jane whether she was angry with him for something, and Jane admitted that Alicia had told her about "the angry things" Sean had said about her.

Ultimately, both of them spoke to a facilitator, actually the person who had taught the class on conflict resolution, and they all agreed to ask Alicia to meet with them. During that meeting, Jane and Sean spoke openly with Alicia about her triangulated message. As Sean said afterward, in this corporation it was up to him to confront Jane when he was ready to do so and not have his comments carried by someone else. Alicia apologized, and said she would try not to triangulate in the future. Jane bought a set of earphones, and the corporate value was learned once again.

This guideline plays an important role in management. It stops third-party messages from being used by a supervisor. They know they need to directly experience a problem behavior to use it in supervision.

Does such work take a lot of time? Yes. And we have found that it reduces future conflict and increases the sense of safety between employees at work. It's worthwhile work.

Diversity is an RHD asset. The goal of the corporation is to appreciate the uniqueness in each of us, and to embrace those differences in all of us. How does this happen?

- By developing self-awareness within employees. To value our individual selves and to value others is the goal. We all have biases, but an awareness of those biases can serve as the "red flag" that help us consciously avoid behaving toward others in ways that are based on biased attitudes.
- By affirming our differences. Holding multi-cultural events to celebrate who we are and the differences we illustrate, is an on-going activity.
- By rejecting discriminatory behaviors in recruitment, hiring, and other employment practices.
- By creating systems to vigorously investigate and resolve allegations of discriminatory practices and negating behaviors.

When we create an environment in which each person's uniqueness is valued, honored and appreciated, we have the opportunity to bring out the best in each of us. And this, in turn, enriches the life of the organization.

EVERY DAY OF MY ENTIRE LIFE

In light of racism as an American reality, the RHD meeting that occurred in July of 2005 was a miracle – the kind of miracle that can happen when human beings ready themselves for it. About forty people were packed into the room for the meeting, and each one was listening closely to Mary, the new Unit Director of an RHD service in Tennessee, as she spoke over the speakerphone. It was about an African-American employee named George.

"George looked upset when he walked into the office," Mary said, "and he reported the following incident: He was at a local site for developmentally delayed people, sitting in a room with Chris, a white office manager, while she was trying rather unsuccessfully to manage a distraught mother on the phone. When Chris hung up she sniped, 'I'm not going to talk to her if she acts like a stupid nigger.'

"George usually kept things to himself, but this time he told me about the incident, and I suggested that he, Chris and I meet the next morning. Then I called Paula, my Hub Leader in Philadelphia, for coaching."

Paula picked up the story line: "In RHD we see such an incident as a conflict, this time between Chris and George. The first step is to try to help them work it out. 'You may end up firing Chris,' I said to Mary, 'but then again, you might end up thinking that she can learn another kind of behavior.' And then we talked about how to hold the meeting…."

Mary continued, "As it turned out not only was Chris disrespectful of George in the meeting, she actually admitted to making the racist comment. And all the while, she kept putting words in George's mouth. 'Don't you remember I said that I didn't mean any insult? You understand how frustrating that woman is…'

"George had to bellow his response over her voice: 'I'm an adult. You don't have to speak for me. I can speak for myself! Every day of my life I have to remind people I am an adult.' "

"In short," Mary said, "Chris didn't have the interpersonal skills necessary for her job, nor did she show any interest in learning how to control her hostile behavior. So I fired her that day with the full support of Paula, my Hub manager."

Paula recalls that members of the group sitting in that room, until then silent, began to talk about racist comments made at work, in particular those expressed by RHD's consumers. "People understood that this is complicated because our consumers are mentally ill and/or developmentally disabled, intellectually limited and/or socially inept. However, the fact remained: our African-American staff was being subjected to racist and abusive behavior from the very people they were caring for. And then a woman in the group offered the way ahead: 'Let's get some training set up so we can learn how to respond to racism when it happens in RHD.' "

Stimulated by this meeting, the Racism Committee is now holding a series of discussions on how to respond to and professionally manage the racist comments of our consumers, as well as the racist comments of employees. It's too early to know what will result from these discussions, but I believe that consumers are with us to learn appropriate social skills. They, too, need to be guided by our values. And those who make racist comments need the attention of our behavior specialists, our case managers, and our trained staff. There's much work to be done.

Racism is so prevalent in our society it is naïve to think it will disappear from our corporation. We can, however, endeavor to address it with strength and forthrightness in our own corporate cultures.

CHAPTER IV

RHD VALUES AND CORPORATE SUCCESS

In the last chapter we talked about the equal human worth assumption underpinning RHD values that highlight respect and equality in the workplace. Employees learn, and are expected to use these values to guide them at work. In particular, we focused on how employees manage conflict.

In this chapter we focus primarily on the impact of the second assumption, that people are essentially good, although the other two assumptions – that people are of equal human worth and there is no one way to run a corporation well – are also examined. Recall, we have said that these assumptions lead the corporation to delegate vast amounts of authority to local workgroups. Now we look at how the values that emerge from these assumptions offer workgroups the freedom and the responsibility to shape their jobs. We find them debating work issues, managing budgets (with financial oversight), being creative, and questioning authority. And when the opportunity arises, we also see them extending our values-based approach to issues in the larger community.

RHD is very deliberate in establishing the guidelines we believe are essential to workgroup and, thus, corporate success. We are mindful of continually referring to, revising, and implementing our values and our *Bill of Rights and Responsibilities* as part of our ongoing effort to keep our culture directly related to our values. I learned the importance of such a workplace culture – and the danger of its absence – very early in my work life.

During my college years in New York City, I spent three weeks working in a plastics fabrication plant making small plastic bags for the low-end cosmetics industry. My Hispanic fellow workers weren't as fortunate; they were locked into this work for years, perhaps lifetimes.

I was struck by the existence of a time clock situated near the front door. To get paid, I had to make sure to clock in and clock out every day. I was intrigued, captivated by the clock. It was a symbol; of what, initially I was not sure, but I noted that management did not use the clock.

Why was it used, I wondered? I was certain that this was a prevailing practice in factories across the country. After all, administrators had to make sure that the workers were paid accurately, and I had no doubt that there were workers who would lie about the hours spent on the job if they were trusted to fill in the hours on paper. Nevertheless, that clock bothered me in this factory with eighteen employees. Still, I had no ability to question it.

Now I understand what the act of punching in on that clock meant to me and to my fellow workers – namely, that our supervisors didn't trust us. That wasn't the only problem in the factory. We workers knew our managers got perks and benefits that were denied to us. On hot days we ate our lunch sitting on a fire escape trying to get a few breaths of cool air. Our managers sat in air-conditioned offices because their work demanded better "concentration." The verbal abuse gratuitously meted out reminded us that the factory also had a hierarchical structure, and we were at the bottom. As I look back, I can only conclude that this factory achieved the questionable goal of producing the highest level of worker anger and the least amount of worker energy conceivable.

I lasted about three weeks before being fired. I don't recall whether they had less need for workers or I just didn't learn how to manage the foot press fast enough. Being fired, however, was a relief.

The time clock stayed in my mind. And years later, when someone suggested using that kind of mechanism at RHD, I realized there was an obvious alternative: workers could simply use pen and paper to sign in and out, indicating the time next to their signature. And working groups could be small enough for supervisors to know and respond to the time needs of individual employees. People don't have to be treated as though they are simply cogs in a machine.

Why use a mechanism that communicates a lack of trust in the honesty of employees? Why not find a way to communicate trust? Over the years, I have heard many managers argue, "What difference would it make? The time clock is only for line workers. And even if they didn't have to punch in, they would still receive low wages. They would still have little hope for a better job." Now I know how to answer them.

Treating employees as cogs in a machine, whether through the use of a time clock or any other de-humanizing practice, makes an enormous difference. It moves a corporation toward distrusting everybody. To counter that tendency within RHD, if we need rules I ask myself how can we create them so that they apply to everyone equally? And what kind of processes will expand the trust between people? I've had enough experience to know that expanding trust, and creating as much equality as possible, goes a long way toward generating corporate success.

The effort is an optimistic, expansive, and open-minded approach to business that, we have demonstrated, results in a spectacularly positive bottom line. Many of its components are delineated in the *Bill of Rights and Responsibilities*. The one we focus on first is essential to our expectation that workgroups will be able to manage the multiple perspectives that arise in any small group and thus debate their own work issues.

> ...expanding trust, and creating as much equality as possible, goes a long way toward generating corporate success.

ENCOURAGING MULTI-LEVEL THINKING

One salient aspect of RHD's corporate culture is that we expect employees can learn how to work with multiple perspectives, or multi-level thinking, and so debate workgroup issues. It is one of our official values and is listed as such in our *Bill of Rights and Responsibilities*. The roots of multi-level thinking, of course, are in our second and third assumptions – that people are essentially good and there is no one way to manage corporate issues well.

We believe the creative chaos arising from multiple perspectives is of great worth. Such chaos is not seen as formless confusion, but as a dynamic tension and ferment that leads to fresh ideas and leaps of creativity. Pulling these perspectives together offers a richness that can't be duplicated in one person.

Multi-level thinking is also a tool for dealing with workplace conflict, whether it is about how to deal with an uncooperative colleague or a consumer who is resistant to healthcare. Since diversity of opinions is likely in any small workgroup, each person is seeing an issue from a slightly different slant. So to speak, it is a healthy problem that can lead to very creative actions.

...chaos is not seen as formless confusion, but as a dynamic tension and ferment that leads to fresh ideas and leaps of creativity.

People at RHD talk about the importance of accepting multiple perspectives in a workgroup, and also about using the both/and thinking we introduced in Chapter I. Both/and thinking, remember, transcends the narrow "either/or" perspective that divides knowledge into a simplistic calculation of right and wrong or true and false, but instead accepts and promotes a balance between the two, or some kind of third way that to some degree satisfies all participants. Of course, not all workgroup members have the capacity for multi-level or both/and thinking – but it is likely that some members will, thus shaping the debate.

A manager tells the following story about multi-level thinking and both/and solutions:

> *"I recall sitting with a development group that was debating how to write a proposal in response to a governmental request for proposals that was very poorly funded. Group members had two markedly different approaches to the task; some wanted to offer the trimmed-down, less than adequate service that government wanted – at minimal cost. They felt strongly that we had to give government what they wanted. Others felt sure that the project couldn't be done at that minimal cost, that if we tried we would fail and RHD's reputation would suffer. Given the strong feelings on each side, we used a facilitator. I watched while she gave each side plenty of air space and then asked for some both/and thinking. But neither side moved to the middle. Then they found a third way – representatives of each side would test out their bias with their governmental contacts, and then they would try again to use both/and thinking.*
>
> *Several weeks later, the full group had produced one proposal – it was only barely satisfying to both sides. Ultimately, we won the contract, and although it wasn't easy, we created a satisfactory service. And*

government was grateful. The next time that particular arm of government requested a proposal, we opted to write for a more sufficient amount of money – and won that grant as well."

–Harold

How do we promote multi-level and both/and thinking? To begin, over the years in the RHD corporate culture, people have learned to offer active and consistent affirmation to those who express their ideas and concerns. When there is disagreement, we expect everyone will address the issue in a respectful, caring way. And managers use these opportunities to model multi-level and both/and thinking. Also, during meetings I point out how my approach changed due to ideas introduced by someone, and where possible, I emphasize a contribution that came from a line worker. As managers, we urge employees to use facilitators to help them learn these skills, and we encourage people to try things they've never tried before, or that others say are impossible. We stay aware that silence does not necessarily signify agreement or understanding.

The flip side of promoting multi-level thinking is discouraging behaviors that interfere with it. To this end, we educate group leaders not to set agendas for meetings, not to dominate discussions, and not to avoid discussions on issues to be decided. We encourage group members not to withhold their contributions and not to reject the views of others. Our culture is strong enough that sarcasm and other kinds of putdowns are very rare – quickly noted and challenged in groups. And if anyone complains privately about authoritarian decision-making, they are likely to be asked to raise the issue directly with group leaders. If I am involved, I ask people not to let the issue drop.

A perfect example of the benefit of encouraging multi-level thinking happened about a year ago, when two people were fired in the Central Office for theft – one was gay, the other heterosexual. The heterosexual employee instituted a grievance; the committee found in her favor, so she was reinstated. The gay man didn't try to grieve. And then the rumors began. Some of our gay employees felt there was clear evidence of prejudice in the way the two firings were managed. Some heterosexual employees agreed with them. Other gay employees thought the rehiring was correct. Still others spoke of the increased tension in the office, and the fear that "they could be next."

In the RHD culture people offer active and consistent affirmation to those who express their ideas and concerns.

An office staff meeting was held, during which a facilitator wrote for display the many different perspectives that were suggested. As the participants saw the range of perspectives, and discussed how multi-level thinking meant respecting every one of them, the conversation began to mirror the complexity of the problem. Soon cooler heads began to speak, appreciating the facts behind the firings and the rehiring. By the end of the meeting, creativity took hold, and people began to talk about strategies that could be used in the future, including a buddy system for workers in trouble with their supervisors.

Encouraging multi-level thinking diffused the tensions of a potentially explosive situation, engaged employees rather than disempowering them, and resulted in a bottom-up innovation that has continued to prove highly effective.

THE POWER TO QUESTION AUTHORITY

As an outgrowth of our assumption that employees are essentially good, we therefore believe they have something worthwhile to contribute. And, of course, holding the assumption that there can be many good approaches to corporate issues, questioning authority is vital to a common good corporation. We don't mean the rebellious idea that these words often invoke, but the principle, inherent in the process of questioning authority, that everyone benefits from the expression of multiple perspectives – especially if it challenges the status quo. Imagine, if you can, the condition of our world if Nelson Mandela or Thomas Jefferson had not questioned the authority of the systems and thinking of their times. A lack of inquiry can allow mistakes, false assumptions, and erroneous ideas to be perpetuated.

Realistically, a successful corporation requires an environment that fosters and supports constructive challenges. In many cases, an employee's experience may give him or her access to more or better information than possessed by "higher-ups" in the corporation. Questions like: "Why are we doing things this way?" or "Isn't there an easier way to accomplish this task?" signify the kind of ongoing analysis that is key to the vibrancy of RHD and any service that it delivers.

As we often say, it is important to keep the spirit of free debate alive in a corporation striving for the common good. The power to question authority, therefore, is central to RHD's values.

Questioning authority within the context of the workplace, however, must be balanced against the fact that the employer by necessity defines the tasks to be accomplished and the broad conditions within which the work takes place. Accepting a job with a particular employer implies an agreement to accomplish the assigned tasks within those established conditions. And managers and supervisors have the authority to assure that work is completed. This ultimate authority cannot legitimately be dismissed if the organization is to accomplish its mission. *How* the work gets done, however, is quite another matter; here the issue of authority is by no means absolute.

Authority is defined variously as the power to execute dominating control or influence, and the capacity to motivate a small group effort. At RHD, the first definition is rejected. No one, on any level in this organization, has the power to exercise dominating control. In fact, authoritarian leadership that arises anywhere in the corporation needs to be questioned. The second definition of authority – the capacity to motivate a small group effort – is important in the RHD culture.

The type of authority that RHD seeks to foster is that which comes with direct experience and the expertise that arises with it. Certainly, education and training add to that expertise – but direct experience is usually essential. Each aspect of the corporation's operations is populated with individuals who have developed and demonstrated expertise in the area of their work endeavors. It lends weight to the counsel and advice these people bring to the workplace. Does this mean the counsel and advice is not to be questioned? Absolutely not. Even the best leaders are, after all, human beings without absolute knowledge of how to solve corporation issues. Dissent is a valuable source of creativity.

One small but meaningful way we promote our culture of meaningful, independent dialogue at RHD is a red button with the words "Question Authority" in bold black letters. People wear them on their clothes. I keep a supply of them on my desk, freely hand them out, and enjoy the process. I am aware of how often that basket needs to be refilled. In fact, as I write this, my

> No one, on any level in this organization, has the power to exercise dominating control.

assistant is executing an order for another 500. The button reminds employees to ask for clarifications, to offer alternative perceptions, and certainly to challenge anything that doesn't make sense.

That employees will use this "license to question" to undermine the authority of management is a worry of some of my colleagues – some of whom are RHD leaders. I understand that they feel somewhat awkward. But I believe that unquestioned authority is always more dangerous than undermined authority, in particular for a corporation that aims to be at the cutting edge.

One of the Central Office staff tells the following story about an RHD leader who knew how to listen closely to her staff:

> *When I first visited the Main Street shelter for men, which was shortly after its management was shifted to us from another social agency, I recall saying hello to a staff member and being shocked by the anger in his eyes. He looked as if he was on the edge of a scream or a fight – it was clear he expected to be poorly treated. And then there were the homeless men sitting listlessly in rows of metal chairs. They looked beaten down, isolated and dreary. When I returned the second time, RHD had been running the shelter for about a year. Recalling my first visit, I made a point of looking into the eyes of staff. Much to my delight, there was a smile in many of their eyes. The homeless men looked more at ease, less isolated from each other. I knew this was the result of values-based leadership and the development of a culture that released kindly and productive staff energy. From the outside it looked like a miracle.*
>
> *–Jennifer*

OPEN COMMUNICATION

Open communication is another corporate value that springs from trust in our employees, our rejection of rigid authoritarian structures, and our assumption that there are many ways of looking at issues. Open communication – simply put – means two things in RHD:

- Anyone (or any group) can speak with anyone else in the entire corporation directly about anything at all at any time.
- No one is permitted to use their "authority" to prohibit the open and free communication of ideas or concerns any employee may wish to express.

To say that this is an aspect of our corporate culture sets us apart from many other businesses. It is true that in RHD, as in all other work environments, there are defined lines of authority. Each of us has a "boss." In most companies, however, all communication of ideas and/or issues is required to flow up this "chain of authority" to some higher place at which decisions are or are not made. Such communication frequently gets blocked, changed, or lost somewhere along the chain, often by a supervisor who is either indifferent or fearful.

Consequently, many workers choose to stifle creative ideas rather than risk the disapproval of their supervisors. They may speak "unofficially" to other co-workers about their concerns, suggestions, and ideas, but they may be hesitant to express them to their "boss." When an employee in such a corporation does speak directly to a supervisor, it's likely that his or her ideas will be rejected or dismissed. And they see no positive results. If they think there is no place else to go – no alternative – then discontent and/or apathy emerge and, too often, great ideas are lost.

We decided early in our corporate history that we did not want such a rigid structure regarding human communication. Our written Values Statement speaks about the "open environment" we promote. That means that when the ordinary "chain of authority" venue is felt to be ineffective by an employee – for whatever reason – that employee is welcome to choose another venue of communication. He or she may speak respectfully with anyone at any level of the corporation and expect some response or resolution to the issues presented – in a reasonable time frame. That's important for the continued health of our organization.

As you will see in Chapter V we have developed many opportunities for this communication – small group meetings that undertake specific corporate-wide efforts including the Values Committee itself. And staff is encouraged to participate in these discussions. In regard to personal work problems, obviously it is recommended that an employee first approach his or her immediate supervisor, since that is the way most issues can be most rapidly addressed. When that approach is not sufficient or comfortable, all employees are encouraged to identify another person or persons with whom they can share their insights, and who will follow through with appropriate actions. In summary, *no one* in RHD is empowered to prohibit open communication between members of our corporate community. We take open communications very seriously in our corporate culture; breaches tend to be dealt with in ways that also bring in the value, previously described, of Questioning Authority – and the communicator is protected by our whistleblower policy.

A member of the Payroll Department tells of the following incident:

> *"A newly hired Manager of Payroll, having spent many years in corporate America, called a meeting during which he asked us to make sure that all communication to other departments went through him. He was surprised at how quiet the room became right after he spoke. After a few uncomfortable moments, someone said; "We've never operated that way. Perhaps, before you make such a change, you should check it out with your supervisor."*
>
> *–Sarah*

This new administrator made the mistake of assuming that the best way for his department to function was through centralized communication. This was, however, counter to RHD's emphasis on open communication – indeed, it's an established employee *right*. When the administrator issued an order in contradiction of this right, one of the staff used another RHD right – Questioning Authority – to do just that. In doing so, this staff member made the *Bill of Rights and Responsibilities* come alive.

QUALITY WORK

What is quality work? I suggest that it is a certain characteristic; you might call it a flavor, of certain people when they're at work. While that flavor is difficult to define, it can be sensed in the easy flow of productive activity, in the smiles and the good humor of people doing the work – it seems to be easy, they appear to be having fun. And somehow serious intent and good humor are joined together.

How does quality emerge? Here's an example from a line worker:

I grew up as a foster care child in Philadelphia. It wasn't an easy life, and perhaps as a result, I feel for people who look lost – people like Bobbie who had a rough life. Tall, gaunt and usually in a daze, he was diagnosed as having a limited intelligence as well as a mental illness. When I first met him, in an RHD shelter, he was also illiterate. And like so many others who can't read or write, ashamed of his inability. I felt drawn to him; he also grew up as a foster care child in Philadelphia.

"His illiteracy first showed up when he couldn't fill out a form for a laundry inventory. So I began to teach him how to read by cutting out pictures of things – a shirt, a pair of pants, a comb, -- writing their names underneath the picture and pasting them near where he kept those things. He was a guy who hung out around the shelter. I thought at first he liked being with the staff, but then I learned it was because he had no means of transportation. He couldn't travel by bus because he couldn't read bus signs. So we rode the buses together; he sounded out the names of the streets and finally learned where to get off – and how to get back home. I was real proud of Bobbie – he was a quick learner."

–Susan

Conditions were ripe for this quality story: Susan's unit was imbued with the assumption that people are essentially good. And because they also understood that there is no one way to do corporate work, every employee could contribute. This led to a safe and open workplace, and an empowered workgroup. In it, Susan had the freedom to make her own workplace decisions, and so she developed the heartfelt relationship she had with Bobbie. While their relationship grew out of their similar past, another, less obvious, trigger was present: quality care is a human capacity that naturally arises – when conditions are right.

Quality care is a human capacity that naturally arises – when conditions are right

Unfortunately, managers in the typical corporation see quality in a markedly different way – as a thing that can somehow be *isolated* and then *injected* into corporate work. These managers also believe that quality can be measured. So surveys abound in an effort to tag this "thing" called quality. There is a belief that it can be found in the results of a work effort – perhaps positive statements from consumers – and then injected into other workgroups. But quality isn't a thing – so it cannot be measured and it cannot be injected. Instead, it is a characteristic, a feeling of the work in a community of people who are free to be creative and caring.

Sometimes typical corporations produce practices that make the conditions that produce quality very unlikely. As an example, consider the many corporations that automatically create job descriptions for all their employees. RHD consciously does not use this tool. Instead, the assumption that people are essentially good leads us to believe that, once an employee has a general sense of the job, he or she will want to shape the way it is done – and then go on to use their freedom to find the flavor of quality.

Thelma, for instance, had already been working as a receptionist at our new outpatient clinic for many years when she asked me for a job description. I responded quickly saying that her job required that she arrive at work at 8:00 A.M. and from there on it was up to her to do what she felt was needed for that day. I felt, and so told her, that it was absurd for me to define the details of her work since she was already doing a quality job. One of her outstanding behaviors was the kindness with which she greeted our clients, brought them coffee, and made sure that the therapists took them into the therapy room in a timely manner. Delineating her kindness was impossible; words would never have done justice to her heartfelt warmth. Thelma already knew how to perform her job and a detailed job description, I believed, would have done her more harm than good.

The problem with a job description is that a supervisor, who believes that he or she can fully enumerate the tasks needed, may inadvertently diminish quality, given the tendency of employees to give supervisors only what they want. Besides, there is no single way to define a job, and no supervisor has *the* answer to how another person's job should be performed. If, as Thelma's supervisor, I imposed my view of her job, the corporation would, in effect, lose her special contribution – her way of managing the relationship between people. That would have been a great loss.

In summary, quality work is an outcome of many of our values – safe and open workplaces, empowered groups, decentralized authority, the freedom to question authority, and the vibrant energy that a community of working colleagues can generate when they have the freedom to be creative. Indeed, quality work is closely related to every RHD value. Why? Because all the values are designed to offer freedom as well as responsibility. The development of a common good corporation is, by its very nature, an opportunity for quality work through community building in the workplace.

IMPLEMENTING THE VALUE OF CREATIVITY

Creativity is another value, one so intrinsic to the common good corporation that it is listed in the *Bill of Rights and Responsibilities*, and is a clear outgrowth of our trust in our employees. Under this banner, employees are empowered to promote new directions. A group of employees can suggest that the corporation pursue any new project if the idea benefits those around them and/or society in general, and if they have, or can figure out how to get, the funds to try it. They also need to have the energy and the commitment to pursue the idea, and be willing to take the personal *risk* in implementing the idea. Last but not least, the project must be legal.

I am particularly gratified when that creativity is directed toward the larger community. No corporation exists in a vacuum; RHD is affected by the communities that surround it and, in turn, affects them. Therefore in the search for the common good, RHD is particularly tuned into what goes on outside of its corporate boundaries. In fact, our boundaries are very permeable, which means that much seemingly irrelevant information comes in and goes out. Some might think this is a waste of time, but that's not my experience.

Here are a few examples of how permeable and even open boundaries lead to the creativity that benefits both communities and the corporation.

- Staff will often alert management to broader social issues that concern them. Recently, one such comment led the Central Office to continue buying heating oil from a community cooperative even though, that year, we could have bought it for a lower price. As a result, we helped the cooperative survive.

- Corporate openness to social issues that are seemingly unrelated to current activity also makes it easy for staff to talk directly to governmental representatives. We tune into their problems and so engage in mutually beneficial problem solving. Sometimes corporate opportunities arise from these conversations, but that's because of mutual interest rather than self-interest alone. I recently happened to meet a unit director who proudly told me that she invited her local city council representative to visit. I complimented her for reaching out on her own to make this happen, and for realizing that connecting with government is important. In many other corporations, she might very well have been criticized for not letting top management know (read: getting permission) before taking the action.

- Corporate openness also stimulates internal discussion. When a staff member observes a gap in services, products, or community needs, that information is likely to be introduced in a corporate meeting. This may result in a stimulating discussion or, perhaps, a new corporate opportunity. I have observed that at least every ten years RHD starts down a major new path, which then results in more than 30% of our activity during the next ten years. And no one could have predicted it at the time. Somebody had to say, "I think there's a need which we can address." Many others had to support the effort even though they couldn't predict the future.

- Many years ago, RHD collaborated with a lawyer to sue a state because mentally ill patients living in state hospitals were working without pay. While we received a good deal of our funds from this state, we embraced this lawyer and his effort. The legal action made sense given our belief in the equal worth of people, including the mentally ill. The lawyer won the case, and, in so doing, changed work practices across the state's mental hospital system. And we didn't lose any of this state's business. I am proud that RHD took that risk. It was true to our values and was an action worthy of a common good corporation.

At its very core RHD's extremely productive culture is built on, among other things, our belief in the essential goodness of people. Why expect untrustworthy people to participate in governing themselves? Why ask them to question authority? It would seem foolhardy. Instead, the focus would be in top-down governance and instituting a wide range of security measures.

And yet not every employee is worthy of the trust we start out with. It is for this reason that our second assumption – "people are basically good" – needs its caveat: "unless proven otherwise." There have been far fewer occasions than one might assume in which invoking that caveat has been necessary. Yet there have been times when our trust in others has been abused. And then many people ask, "Isn't it time to face the fact that we have to protect ourselves? Isn't it time to modify our open and trusting corporate life?"

IS EVERYBODY A CROOK?

Maria[2] was a likeable woman. Just about everyone enjoyed her dry, quick-witted humor, and when there was a party, we could depend on the sound of her bubbly voice to make us laugh. For about ten years she worked for RHD managing the purchasing of office supplies as well our growing fleet of corporate cars. Needless to say, she had our trust.

---

[2]The name and details have been changed for reasons of confidentiality.

I was shocked and saddened when I heard that she committed corporate fraud. And it felt so unnecessary. It seems that her son, who was away at college, needed a car. So Maria loaned him one of ours. It took about two months for us to learn about this. Two days later she was fired. If Maria had asked for some help before she took the car, if she had explained her problem, RHD could have helped out. And, I believe, we would have done so.

In the small town that is our office, I have learned that it's best to be open and direct about important information, otherwise it's likely to become distorted as rumors rule the day. So our Chief Operating Officer and I quickly called a full staff meeting and announced the decision to fire Maria. And then a dark cloud settled over the office. People were stunned. Some wondered how Maria could have done such a thing. Others wished there was a way she could redeem herself. They asked, couldn't we forgive her? After all, she was a member of the RHD "family."

The firing exposed a sometimes forgotten corporate reality. Despite the generally friendly feeling in the Central Office, RHD is a place of work. And certain behaviors cannot be allowed in the public sphere. RHD is a non-profit corporation and management is accountable to our Board, the public, and our funders for all the funds we administer. We need to feel assured that the people who work for us are honest and responsible.

At an even deeper level, Maria's action did damage to the culture that holds us together. That culture is a storehouse of information within which all of us at RHD live. You can't see the information because it's encoded in behaviors. But employees who live within our culture long enough get to "know" it. For instance, they know that it's acceptable to "question authority" in a respectful way, but it's unacceptable to tell "Polish" jokes. Employees are familiar with standards and practices that are not in writing and rarely discussed, such as our diversity of dress and a friendly atmosphere. Our culture is the "self" of the organization, our personality. As such it gives the corporation a sense of coherence and of unity even in our diversity.

RHD's culture is vulnerable. Based as it is on information or ideas, sometimes it feels as unstable as a puff of smoke. We can injure our own culture. Someone like Maria, who steals from us, makes it a little less likely that we will trust each other. That makes RHD a little less safe for the rest of us. Another employee who explodes with anger at a supervisor does the same by ripping apart our understanding that it's possible to patiently work with conflict until we find our way through. From the outside, these attacks are even more frequent; unscrupulous vendors can overcharge; governments can cut funding. There's no doubt about it, we are vulnerable to those attacks.

So we had our reasons for firing Maria, but there are other dangers lurking within this story. Because her behavior exposed RHD's vulnerability to this kind of theft, it raised certain questions within the office: Were other employees also using corporate property for personal use? Should management set up a system to check the location of all corporate cars weekly or daily? Should we ask all unit directors who manage cars across the country to attest in writing that the cars are not being used for personal business?

The danger was, and is, that Maria's theft could lead to a change in RHD's culture – and that those who fear our commitment to trust would succeed in placing corporate security above our belief in the essential goodness of human beings. It's very easy to reduce the level of trust that fills RHD with life and creativity.

The essential question is: should we respond to one instance of corporate theft by lowering the bar of trust, and in so doing treat 3,000 people as though they too might be thieves? Should we let one employee's bad judgment have an even greater impact on the corporate culture by creating procedures that reflect distrust? Should we shift the culture so as to make the realm of distrust larger?

Many administrators in corporate America would say yes to those questions. They would call it "facing reality." At the root of this position is the all-too-common assumption that people cannot be trusted. And, given the human tendency to fear what they do not know, the implication that follows is that no one can be trusted. This is usually justified by the idea that, first and foremost, the corporation must be protected. And then protective, non-trusting procedures are almost automatically instituted.

At RHD, we say "no" to lowering our level of trust. Besides protecting the entity called the corporation, we must also protect a culture that's based on our belief in the worth, dignity, and honesty of each employee.

In the end, RHD did not lose any money. Maria returned the car. All of which brings us to this essential fact: RHD has managed $1.433 billion in government funds over the past thirty-six years, and we can identify only about $ 325,000 in corporate theft that was perpetrated by individuals. That's a loss factor of .00023.

All of us in management work hard to treat our fellow employees well, trusting in their essential goodness. That very belief multiplies the energy that people bring to work. Distrust does the opposite.

CHAPTER V

CENTRALIZE WHAT YOU MUST
AND DECENTRALIZE WHAT YOU CAN

Now that I have described the system of values that inspires Resources for Human Development, we can look at how power is managed through the structure of the corporation. As you will see, both centralization and decentralization have their place. Legal, regulatory, and fiduciary responsibilities tilt us toward centralization while decentralized groups become the powerful corporate motor that allows everyone – workers and consumers alike – to thrive.

The reality is that centralized decision-makers simply don't have enough information to manage the specifics of corporate life. But because centralization is an idea in good currency, corporations generally apply the model haphazardly, in a buckshot attempt to solve almost every problem. In so doing, power is amassed among the very few at the top, rigid hierarchies are developed, workers lose their freedom while productivity eventually slows down. Perhaps the most insidious effect of all is that what could be an involved, energetic work force becomes an angry, resistant and fearful set of workers.

In RHD I find myself spending considerable time arguing for decentralization, perhaps because the centralized model has such absurdly good press in our business culture. Almost every time RHD faces an organizational problem, someone is likely to say, "This is an issue the Central Office needs to solve." Or again, "This is serious, the Central Office has to mandate a solution." These habitual, unthinking responses deny the reality that each time the corporation is moved toward the centralized option, we chip away at the local empowerment that decentralization brings with it. We do well when we find the balance that works best for a particular corporate challenge.

I believe that all corporations can benefit from this approach to governance. It's a big leap, but a highly desirable one, once the advantages are sampled. Dale, one of RHD's Unit Directors, is an example of a manager who benefited from our decentralized model, and then offered it to a group of his staff.

...decentralized working groups become the powerful corporate motor that allows everyone – workers and consumers alike – to thrive.

Let me tell you about our self-directed work team in a day center/art studio that we call Outside the Lines. I have always had immense respect for the use of art as a therapeutic medium, so when we were funded to open a day program, I hired a staff that had that vision. And when the art teachers suggested that they become a self-directed work team, we worked together to make it happen. To this day, that team is responsible for the total operation, including tasks as ordinary as scheduling, and tracking both the census and the budget. They are also responsible for the artistic content of the program, its displays, and its public relations. Leadership has never been assigned; it has emerged naturally over the years as one or another person assumes management responsibilities. The good news is that I don't ever have to say no to art teachers. They join together in groups to make management decisions. However, it's not easy for people to function this way, and sometimes they fail at it. But as long they want to try, we work toward that end

– Dale

Exactly how does this corporate structure work? The quick response is that we centralize when government, legal or financial systems require it. Beyond that we decentralize wherever we can, primarily through unitizing or decentralizing both fiscal and programmatic decision-making.

A DECENTRALIZED STRUCTURE
A Unitized Fiscal System

All corporations require a fiscal system through which information is gathered, processed, centralized and reviewed, and reports are generated for billing and tracking, as well as a yearly audit. At the same time, RHD unitizes or decentralizes this same fiscal system to provide the data units need to make their own local budgetary decisions, whether about hiring, purchasing or offering raises (see Chapter VIII.)

For this to happen the Central Office separately tracks and accounts for *each* funded program contract; currently this includes nearly 1,500 separate divisions of our general ledger. Unit management frequently refers to their subunit of the general ledger, using it as an anchor for decision-making. They are also expected to share the data with staff.

This dispersion of information, and the consequential dispersion of power to make fiscal decisions, creates quite a challenge for corporate leadership. But recall, the common good corporation benefits from the series of small communities that find their energy in face-to-face contact. Units are motivated to keep their budgets in balance or better, and the corporation as a whole gets a happier, engaged workforce and a better product.

To be successful these local managers must thoroughly understand, and fulfill, the contracts under which they operate. It is clear that a Unit cannot operate in deficit without permission from top corporate leadership. However, unit managers are not alone in this complex effort. The central office hires budget managers to guide them. And everyone is aided by established fiscal procedures, including the expectation that monthly reports be timely and accurate. We also have safety nets including the one that comes with the requirement that any check over $5,000 be counter-signed by the COO.

As long as a unit stays within budget or produces surplus income, local managers have the freedom to be innovative. Responsible fiscal management has become a source of pride at RHD. During our 37 years and over $1.3 billion in revenue, we have never lost a contract due to fiscal mismanagement. Now over 200 directors in 11 states and Washington D.C. make these decisions.

A Unitized Program System

While RHD began as one unit, over the years it has become a series of semi-autonomous, decentralized units that are related to the center through the fiscal system, program support and oversight, as well as a range of informal relationships. For a couple of decades we were small enough to rely primarily on these informal relationships. About ten years ago, however, when we realized

> As long as a unit stays within budget or produces surplus income, local managers have the freedom to be innovative.

RHD needed more cohesion, the corporation sub-divided into working groups called Hubs.

As the structure exists now, there are thirteen Hubs. Each offers both fiscal and programmatic oversight for a number of units totaling between $8-12 million in activity each year. To coordinate this effort, Hub leaders expect to be kept informed of major potential or existent problems, and top management expects Hub leaders to keep them informed.

In most cases, however, centralized Hub personnel do not expect to solve unit problems. Why? Because parallel to this centralized oversight structure is the unit structure with managers whose job it is to solve potential or existing problems. Hub staff may advise and even help, but at their best, they do not move in to control a unit unless a problem arises that is deemed to threaten the corporation.

Hubs are composed of units offering an array of services for diverse populations. One Hub may have a unit that provides residential care of mentally ill adults in a particular state, and a shelter for the homeless in a second state. Since no one person at the Hub level can know all this detail, the expertise needed to provide services remains decentralized, spread across a range of local managers. In this way, we avoid cookie-cutter uniformity and corporate blandness.

Hub personnel are engaged in varied activities. They work with well-established units and with units that are just getting started. They can be responsible for a unit undergoing a change in leadership and support another unit's expansion. This makes life less orderly, less predictable, and more interesting for everyone.

ACTIVITIES THAT TILT TOWARD DECENTRALIZATION

Local purchasing is guided by unit budgets, which in turn are based on contracts with our funders (generally, these are the government agencies who engage us to provide services to populations in need). With the help of budget managers (Central Office employees), local staffs furnish living spaces, outfit offices, and buy food and household supplies for or with consumers. In some cases the cost of those locally bought purchases runs somewhat higher than if bought centrally, but our corporate gain far outweighs these costs because of our

> ...at their best [Hubs] do not move in to control a unit unless a problem arises that is deemed to threaten the corporation.

goal – that local employees and our clients feel trusted and empowered.

Local hiring and firing empowers unit management. While our Human Resources Department is responsible for providing training, support, and education of unit personnel regarding employment practices, they do not provide a centralized hiring process. We are structured this way because we believe that, for a cohesive identity, units need to be actively engaged in the selection of new members. Corporate management reinforces this cohesion by asking unit leaders to include workers in hiring decisions.

The firing process is more complex; indeed it is one of the more difficult challenges leaders and their working groups face. If it isn't handled well, feelings can run high, legal challenges may emerge, and group performance suffers. Given these potential problems, corporate management asks that firing be a process that results from progressive supervision, and that at minimum it be a two-person decision. While I am often personally distressed by how long it takes for a supervisor to fire an incompetent employee, I am proud when it is evidence of the concern felt at the prospect of depriving a person of a salary.

A local design for client care is created by those doing the work. It is obvious that work plans should make sense to, and get the buy-in from those who must execute them. When worker empowerment is the operating mantra, quality work is more likely.

Certainly Central Office Hub members provide support and assistance. And our Access Team, a Central Office function, offers training and education, coaching and organization development consultation. In the example below, local managers made decisions during the Katrina hurricane that people at a distance could never have made. They were remarkably successful in caring for our consumers and our staff.

> *I believe we were successful because we didn't have an RHD-Philadelphia crisis protocol. It would have been easy for a manager in the Central Office to come up with a list of things to do. But they didn't, which meant we could come up with our own plans. And that meant we did just what we thought we needed to do, rather than following someone else's procedure. Our focus was on supporting our staff so we worked with all the people out on the streets that needed our care.*

While I am often personally distressed by how long it takes for a supervisor to fire an incompetent employee, at times I am proud when it is evidence of the concern felt at the prospect of depriving a person of a salary.

Every staff member was provided with the opportunity to decide when to come back to work. When they did, some worked longer days so they wouldn't have to commute five days a week. We also made our workdays shorter so, if they had to, they could commute. The effect of all this was that our employees came back sooner – and we were out taking care of our consumers when no one else was. Meanwhile, during every telephone contact with the Central Office, someone asked, is there anything you need?

–Jan

And when worker empowerment is the operating mantra, quality work is more likely.

Local accountability is more likely when small groups are empowered – members then grow to care about each other and the work being done. Supervisors who are in face-to-face relationships with the employees they supervise are also more likely to understand the personal issues affecting those employees – and therefore more likely to accommodate their needs. This adds to the quality of the workgroup experience. And managers who are close to the point of service tend to be effective in a moment of crisis. All this makes quality work more likely.

Recently when I heard from Michael, one of RHD's Associate Directors, that we had terminated the employment of a Unit Director, I asked how did word of this Director's erratic behavior reach Central Office leadership?

The staff became worried when the Unit Director abruptly canceled planned trips for clients without any reason or discussion. Increasingly this Director was also showing a sudden loss of temper, yelling and "bossing others." And staff knew this wasn't the RHD way of leading people. When they saw that the Director's behavior was affecting the care of the families in their charge, a few of them decided to call their Hub leader. The calls triggered an investigation.

The search for new business is the responsibility of entrepreneurs in start-up efforts. We create that entrepreneurial spirit as each new unit chooses its own name, buys its own stationery and develops its own promotional material. Successfully growing units develop their own sense of purpose and pride. Unit Directors build relationships with their governmental customers, and solicit new business opportunities.

The corporation's growth rate is robust because it has many growing points, local leaders who are empowered to make decisions and so can respond to customer need. This effort is so successful that there are as many as a hundred entrepreneurial efforts occurring each day. None of these efforts need to be checked by corporate leadership, but advice and support is always available.

Unit leadership is responsible for satisfying their governmental customers. They are also responsible for reporting problems to managers in the Central Office. While this model works most of the time, on two occasions during the last four years, we had to intervene and withdraw the freedom Unit Directors usually assume is theirs. Given the implications for the corporation, perhaps more serious than the loss of money involved, was that a number of staff reacted with the standard belief that an increased centralized oversight for everyone would prevent these problems in the future.

In my experience, failure almost always triggers the urge to centralize. And the reason is the false perception that centralized oversight, and control, is safer. People believe that it prevents failures. When I hear this idea, I can, and do, refer to the failures that have occurred in large highly centralized corporations such as Enron, Citibank, IBM, and many others. And I also talk about the productive power of our own organizational model. After all, RHD has proven that our emphasis on decentralization is connected to our success. This success is too important to give up because of what are essentially infrequent problems in our corporate history.

ACTIVITIES THAT TILT TOWARD CENTRALIZATION

When government requires a centralized structure. Because centralization is believed to lead to a more efficient and accountable organization, RHD is sometimes asked to combine units and appoint a manager with a broad span of authority – who will then report to government. While our preferred span is approximately fifty staff to one Unit Director, to satisfy our customers we have sometimes doubled or tripled that – and then ask this Director to find ways to empower smaller groups within that larger structure.

> ...each unit chooses its own name... buys stationary and develops its own promotional material.

When unit directors are successful entrepreneurs. A Unit Director's span of authority as well as his or her status and salary increases as expansion occurs. As this happens, the director has less direct contact with the small groups that provide the service. Since the common good corporation values face-to-face management, we expect the director to replicate RHD's design, which means decentralizing decision-making so that it takes place close to the point of service.

When consumer health requires increased services. Given the increasing age or diminishing health of certain consumers, we have created a centralized effort to assess need and support additional care. We also have a centralized clinical review and support of our mental health services, and use professional consultants to teach and consult. Even though these are centralized efforts, we strive to keep the responsibility for final decisions in the unit.

When the corporation is under attack. Given our size, an attack will periodically surface somewhere in the corporation. That demands a centralized response. For example, whenever a consumer dies, whether from natural or other causes, I ask to be immediately notified. I do this both because I want to know of, and evaluate, the situation, but also to be sure that it is managed with the corporate-wide community in mind. This is not business as usual; top management must assess the causes, determine whether others are at risk, and whether the corporation itself is at risk.

When the corporation is under attack, whether for well-founded or spurious reasons, I expect that communication with the outside world, other than families of our consumers or our government customers will be sharply centralized. I can then decide whether to respond or delegate the response.

Several years ago, a seriously disturbed fourteen year-old boy in our care died. The death occurred after our staff physically restrained the child to prevent him from hurting others. After it had been reported in a local newspaper, a team from a local television news channel called wanting to interview me. I agreed knowing that with this "hot" news came the supposition that we mistreated the boy.

I called an impromptu meeting and was briefed on the situation, but handled the TV interview by myself. Much later the coroner's report confirmed that the cause of death was a previously undetected heart condition. When he came to us, only ten days earlier, the child was probably on inappropriate medication. We often take care of people who have received less than adequate health care. Our commitment is to do our best.

AT THE INTERFACE BETWEEN DECENTRALIZATION AND CENTRALIZATION

Unit director freedom and responsibility. There is an interpersonal space between units and the Central Office in which staff need to work out the details of the centralization/decentralization debate. And the devil is in the details. For instance, it would be easy for centralized management to offer its expertise and then actually do what we assume is a unit director function. And it's likely that some directors would welcome that help; it would, after all, reduce their workload. The catch is that such "help" can also be disempowering.

For example, a unit director who is faced with having to fire an employee is likely to ask the advice of RHD's Human Resources group; however, if the advice given is taken as a directive, our decentralized effort is undermined. We localize firing so that people close to the action will make their best decisions and work with the fallout of the action. And so we ask Human Resources' staff to give unit management the information that will empower them, but not to make decisions for them. In this way the boundary between the unit and the central office is maintained. Having learned from this firing, the director will hopefully be able to act rapidly, confidently and decisively, when the next firing is necessary. This is an efficient spread of corporate knowledge and supports decentralization.

Working with the tension at the interface. The centralization/ decentralization debate is ongoing. With a certain frequency staff members wonder: should the job of reporting payroll time be totally processed in each unit or should some of that job happen in the Central Office? Should training and education be mandated or should it be left to unit discretion? Should units have the freedom to create their own clinical services or should the Central Office have a say? And always we're looking for the balance that is both true to our values and programmatically effective. Sometimes that balance tilts toward centralization and at other times toward decentralization.

> The centralization/ decentralization debate is ongoing.

The question is how do we discover that balance point? As a habitual answer neither pole works. And it's important not to get stuck anywhere in the range. In a recent meeting, a Unit Director expressed frustration that the Central Office people who manage our automobiles and insurance told him he had to bring a car that was damaged in an accident to a repair shop that was located 6 miles from his unit. He was frustrated that he had to change from a shop that he was satisfied with, which was 3 blocks from his unit. He took the car to the "suggested" service but also mentioned the issue at one of our periodic Centralization/ Decentralization group discussions, commenting, "This makes no sense to me. I had to use two cars and an extra staff member to make this happen."

When I checked this story out with our fleet manager, he explained, "Many repair services rip off customers and insurance companies. Since we have checked out the legitimacy of the service we recommend, I do think it makes sense to strongly suggest this repair shop." His perspective made sense to me, but rather than setting a firm policy myself, I brought the parties together in our next Centralization/Decentralization meeting. They heard each other's differing viewpoints and decided that, in the future, the repair shop choice would be left to the unit if the car can be driven. It would be left to the fleet manager if it needs to be towed.

Even as I write about the benefits of RHD's centralized and decentralized structure, I'm well aware of the tension that exists between the units and the staff in the central office. It's the push-pull between local freedom and corporate-wide cohesion. And I think that's healthy. After all, it's simply about people trying to be separate and connected at the same time. In corporate life that translates into being a strong and successful unit while also being part of the larger organization.

The tension often runs high in regard to reporting requirements. At the interface, units can assert their freedom by resisting these requirements, while the Central Office can become authoritarian in its requests. RHD employees who understand this dynamic use both/and thinking to allow room for the unit's freedom to question the reporting requirements and Central Office's need to have the data. And then the debate can begin. When that allows for a respectful expression of difference – and if possible a third way – RHD is on the path toward the common good corporation.

A SERIES OF MEETINGS

One strategy for managing the tension between RHD's decentralized units and Central Office managers is through the face-to-face meetings that allow for direct communication. They offer an opportunity for employees to participate in forming and re-forming the corporation. Here are several examples:

The council meeting. Every six weeks this meeting allows anyone in the corporation to register an opinion, suggestion or complaint in front of top management – whether in person or through the use of conference call-in technology. I recall one meeting years ago in which thirty staff members of one program came to this meeting to openly complain in front of their Director about her abusive use of power, all the while knowing that her behavior was in direct contradiction to our corporate values. After getting rapid concurrence from other top managers during that meeting, I limited the Director's ability to fire anyone until we reviewed the complaint. Ultimately, we found for the staff and eliminated her ability to fire or demote employees. It rapidly became quite clear that the Director was abusing our corporate values and should be removed. This was done. Council meetings are a constant source of insight into how our corporation needs to change.

The values meeting. Every two months we hold an open meeting to consider revisions and additions to our *Bill of Rights and Responsibilities*. Recently the group decided to add a section on creativity to the Bill. In an effort to engage as many employees as possible, we devised a corporate-wide contest for creative ideas, developed a selection process and gave four awards during our annual Values Day celebration. Throughout this effort we emphasized that we cannot ever know when and where a new creative idea will be born. This means that leaders must be ready to receive it from anyone, whether that person is a line worker in Louisiana or top management in the Central Office.

The racism meeting. This meeting creates the space for ongoing attention to the relationship between the various races and ethnic groups in the Central Office. Given that racism is a lightning rod in our culture, it's important to expose and explore the tension that staff experiences. Our hope is that over time, each region will have its own racism group.

This effort began after one brief period in 2002 when we had to terminate three African-American staff in the Central Office. Although we employed 149 people in the office at that time, and other layoffs involved white staff, there was a reaction to the three black terminations. Staff openly asked whether skin color had anything to do with the decision. Key people in corporate management, including the African-American members who took part in those terminations, assured the group that skin color did not have anything to do with the decisions.

We decided, however, that this was a time to start what has now become a bi-monthly racism meeting involving me, other members of the management team, and anyone who wanted to raise an issue regarding the perception of racism or any other "ism" in RHD. The discussions range far and wide but occasionally touch on decisions that are difficult to explain. Here are some examples, for instance: "Why is he, a white man, getting a new assignment when I, a black woman, haven't been promoted?" or "I believe that when two black women employees are talking at work, white people think they're wasting time. But if two white workers do the same thing, these same people assume they're talking about work." Now we are starting a discussion group on "The Muslim Voices of RHD". The meetings are a time to evaluate whether some new interventions are possible or necessary to support our commitment to diversity.

The citizen advocates meeting. This group gives a voice to line staff throughout the corporation. In RHD, for every forty employees there must be a citizen advocate elected by the line staff. Now fifty-two of these representatives meet with a Central Office Citizen Advocate Coordinator who also meets monthly with me and other top managers to discuss issues of concern. Both meetings are times when grievances and values can be discussed.

Even though we have an established values document, a formal grievance procedure and open lines of communication, we still need the Citizen Advocates to communicate line staff concerns. Because the Advocates exist, new policies and/or procedures as well as perceived abuses can be reviewed rapidly. I believe that any serious effort at democracy in a corporation that grows beyond fifty employees requires such a system.

I attend all the meetings listed but this last one. Sometimes I envision all this corporate group activity as a series of jazz groups. In each one, musicians play their instruments to interact with each other in a unique performance that takes place across different departments, separate units, and with a wide range of customers. Every once in a while we experience a moment of harmony that resonates across the entire organization. I know that it happens because each and every one of us is exercising our freedom to be creative. In this performance, problems are identified, stakeholder groups are included, and everyone who wants to participate does so. And there isn't a need, or the possibility, for one person to be a controlling conductor!

KATRINA

Getting out of town is no easy matter when you have 43 adults and 24 kids to take care of – and especially if the adults are mentally ill or drug or alcohol addicted. Most had also been homeless prior to entering our community living arrangements.

However, RHD's local staff, which run these residences, rose to the occasion. When the hurricane came close enough to be dangerous, they helped everyone pack, managed residents' (as well as their own) emotional reactions, got them the medication they needed and prepared temporary charts to take along.

And because we were not the legal guardians of these residents, we could not take them unless they wanted to go. So staff talked with each resident about the dangers of the hurricane and helped them to decide whether to go to a family member, to a shelter, or to evacuate with them.

And then there were the decisions about when the unit should leave, where it would go, which employees to take, and whether to take employees' families and pets as well.

Michelle, a Unit Director, described the storm in this way:

> *"As it turned out, Katrina picked up speed as it got closer to land, and suddenly we had to move faster than we thought – that meant making hotel and car reservations twice, once when the storm was further out*

in the Gulf and then when it got very close. That second time meant that I stood on line for hours at the car agency, praying all the time that there would be vans for us and that we would be able to get out of town before the hurricane hit. It was scary. Our initial hotel reservations were in Memphis. However, at the same time that we realized we had to leave town earlier than expected, we also learned that we couldn't get all the new hotel rooms we needed in Memphis. Fortunately, there were rooms available in Dallas, so the group of 3 units split up: Donna and Lori went to Dallas and I went to Memphis – because I had family there who could help out."

Donna, another Unit Director said:

"All three of us, the Unit Directors, worked together to make the evacuation work. We had already learned to share problems and make our own decisions. RHD had taught us that local people must lead the way. Besides, only those who have lived through a hurricane can know what it's like or what needs to be done. Nevertheless, the telephone calls rang back and forth between Philadelphia and New Orleans during the days before landfall. They gave us the financial support we needed; we could never have done this without that as well as their support. We could reach them day and night and talk through any problem we had – but we were the ones who had to actually do it. And then we lost telephone contact. Even the cell phones stopped working. We were really on our own."

Michael, an Associate Director of RHD, recapped his experience:

"We always assumed that the local Unit Directors and their staff would know best what to do. However, I have to admit that if I had been asked where should Michelle's unit go, I would have quickly followed up by asking, 'Where are others going?' I would have suggested that they go to the same place! And because I knew each of the units could and would support each other, and that it would be more efficient to make contact with health care, I would have suggested the three stay together. It was fortunate that I wasn't asked – and that we had taught them well to rely on their own capacity – for staying together was not Michelle's

choice. She went to a different city. And if the truth is told, neither Dallas nor Memphis was the right place to go. There was no simple 'right.'

"While we didn't pull in the reins and centralize control in response to a crisis, we did not simply say it's your call, goodbye. Our support was massive. We were their resource; we thought with them, we found hotel rooms, we offered money. Whenever we could, we helped them get settled in their new cities, which meant establishing contacts for mental and physical health services, getting the necessary prescriptions, etc. And then there was the effort to find friends, family, and other staff and consumers lost in post-hurricane New Orleans. But our help was always in response to a request and in dialogue over the phone."

And Michelle said:

"The result of the decentralized process was spectacular. Staff of many other social agencies in New Orleans took their consumers out of the city and then dropped them off at shelters run by other towns. I know of no other agency that not only evacuated with their consumers but also came back with them. Actually, we never thought there was an alternative to giving them full and continuous care. That's because we were guided by corporate values. They were and are our values. They feed our spirit. And, I believe, that's what helped us get through."

Our experience with RHD's Katrina response only increases my commitment to a decentralized structure. Beyond hurricanes, working groups always face new and challenging decisions. Some of the time routine answers work, but groups and their leaders need to feel free to improvise. As long as actions are taken with the best of intent, we back those innovations and celebrate the work being done. We build the road as we travel.

CHAPTER VI

LEADERSHIP

In the American business culture a Board of Directors delegates the power, which comes in the form of authority over people and money, to run a corporation. Within the for-profit model this is clear: Corporate Boards, which are composed of shareholders and those who represent them, delegate to leadership the authority to manage operations and achieve financial goals. In the non-profit model the boundary between Boards and staff is sometimes not so clear; Boards may not fully delegate the power to run the corporation but may instead remain involved in programmatic and financial management – most likely because its members donate money, and they want more say in how this money is used.

As you will see, the group of citizens who created RHD, and then became its Board of Directors, rejected this intrusive model. Instead they introduced an approach to leadership and power based on trust. This new model began to take form during the winter of 1969 when the group was seeking a mental health professional to lead a new outpatient mental health center. The position was needed to receive a $50,000 government contract.

During my first interview it quickly became apparent that these citizens and I were of the same mind regarding people and their workplaces – and I got the impression that, if they hired me, together we might very well develop an organization that would redesign corporate life as we knew it. Not only did these citizens hire me, they also rejected the traditional non-profit model and gave me the power I needed to run the corporation – while actively contributing their good thinking and full support.

When this new Board and I, the new chief executive officer, began to work together, we quickly and surely agreed on four basic decisions, plus a very explicit understanding: the decisions would hold only so long as corporate revenues equaled or exceeded corporate expenses.

The first decision specified that the Board would not contribute any funds to support corporate general operations. This far-reaching decision laid the groundwork for what would become our common good corporate model. To this day I have never heard of another non-profit that was bound by such a decision.

At the time I barely understood its importance and I certainly did not anticipate how it would shape me as well as the corporation. All I knew was that the staff and I had to rapidly become entrepreneurs. In fact, as soon as we had a place to operate, not only did we produce outpatient services for the mentally ill, we also began to respond to governmental requests for proposals and services. After all, if we didn't make RHD happen, no one would.

The second decision specified that all daily operations would be delegated to the CEO, and through him, to staff; thus highlighting the importance of trust. The rapidity with which this decision was made demonstrated, for me, the clarity and the efficiency that is present when decisions are based on values – in this case, the trust that arises when you believe that people are essentially good unless proven otherwise. Such trust is a cornerstone of the values that we still follow in RHD.

While retaining the power for legal and financial oversight, and the power to review any aspect of corporate activities, to this day the Board does not participate in corporate operations. It has no standing committees and no programmatic agenda. It was clear, the Board had its work and, we, the staff, had our work. The decision had another effect; it allowed me to delegate that same power to local leaders and their small groups – allowing them to do their work.

This Board was also interested in testing new ways to do its own business. I recall that Bertram Wolfson, the Board Chairman, was quick to suggest avoiding the use of Robert's Rules of Order, and instead to base decisions on consensus. This decision changed the tenor of meetings – they were less formal, always

---

The first decision specified that the Board would not contribute any funds to support corporate general operations.

The second decision specified that all daily operations would be delegated to the CEO, and through him, to staff; thus highlighting the importance of trust.

open for staff attendance, and offered more opportunities for an exchange of ideas.

Bert was also quick to reject traditional Board politics and social networking, instead preferring that meetings be focused on the social needs of our client populations. This has led the Board to welcome staff to their meetings. Indeed, groups regularly present their work, thus giving Board members a chance to hear about projects from those who run them and to ask questions about the social and financial issues involved. These practices are still active in Board meetings.

The third decision clarified that the corporation's mission would be broad. The mission could move in many different directions as long as they were each permissible under the IRS regulations applicable to 501(c)(3) non-profit corporations. RHD could stretch the boundaries of its activity; we would not have to limit our efforts to what had been done before by us or by other non-profit organizations.

> The third decision clarified that the corporation's mission would be broad.

Several years after the founding of RHD I recall using this broad definition of our corporate mission to sponsor a local choral group that needed a non-profit home. Staff was excited by the effort – some were musicians who knew how difficult it was for fledgling coral groups to survive. However, at the time there were Board members who couldn't fathom why we wanted to take RHD so far afield. One member particularly thought that such diversity would interfere with our primary focus on mental health services. Quite to the contrary, our diversification and the growth that came with it helped us keep that first clinic functioning through years when funding was scarce. These discussions motivated the Board and RHD leadership to re-commit to our broad mission – if an activity is legal, meets the needs of people, and can be sustained by income, we can pursue it.

> Lastly, the Board asked RHD to develop and maintain a values-led agenda.

Lastly, the Board asked RHD to develop and maintain a values-led agenda. Bert and the Board have always supported the assumption that people are of equal human worth, and that they are essentially good – thus encouraging us to manage the corporation through empowerment and trust. Similarly, Bert and I have always shared the belief that there is no single way to run a corporation –

and that leaders are human and not to be treated as all-knowing beings. This decision motivated us to go further and test how our values can be converted into corporate practices regarding people, power, and money.

And so the formula for common good leadership was put in place. It integrated entrepreneurial pressure, empowerment of others, an open-ended mission, and a series of humanistic values. The formula was used in two ways: to create a locally empowered corporate system, and to generate the people-power needed for success. Indeed, the two are intertwined.

Clearly, this democratic framework was deeply embedded in the group of people who created RHD. But where did they get it? We have already said (see Chapter 5) that the balance of power underpinning the relationship between centralization and decentralization grew out of the American Constitution. But there was another factor involved: when RHD was formed, during mid-twentieth century America, the belief in equality and basic trust were in good currency. It was a clear alternative to the fascism that we had defeated in World War II. Mahatma Gandhi had recently expressed those ideas and Martin Luther King, Jr. was still expressing them. I was awed by what both these leaders had to say.

The group that was creating RHD also knew – and treasured – the tale of a girl named Dorothy and the Wizard of Oz. Perhaps because these characters came into our world through a children's book, the principles of leadership were simple and clear. Frank Baum, the author, believed that people had the capacity to fulfill their human potential, and while there was certainly evil in his fictional world, he assumed good people could subdue it.

Like many a traditional corporate leader, the Wizard of Oz bellowed and roared to frighten people. But when Toto, the dog, pulled aside the curtain that hid his humanity, he was able to admit to his human limitations; indeed he proclaimed himself a bumbling but well-intentioned fool.

For me, Dorothy and the Wizard of Oz are good models for leadership. Like Dorothy, I also include others in our corporate quests. And when I acknowledge my own human limitations by observing that I don't have simple answers to complex problems, I'm replicating the wizard. In fact, Bert and I often join together in comparing ourselves to the Wizard of Oz – in spite of our success we

...the formula for common good leadership became the empowerment of others, an open ended mission, entrepreneurial pressure and a series of humanistic values.

know that we don't have the answers people assume we have. And we know we need to join with others to find the way.

To celebrate the wizard we have created what we call the "Oz Room." It is a curtained enclosure available to anyone who feels the impulse to be authoritarian. With a flip of a switch, the lights flicker, and the person can poke his or her head out of the curtained enclosure to perform like the all-powerful Wizard. We expect that such a leader will figure out that at any time Toto or a fellow employee is likely to expose his or her human foibles.

Most American leaders draw on an undemocratic framework for their work – and I believe that framework stands in the way of corporate success. For this reason, and because it does harm to people, the framework needs to be exposed, at least debated, and preferably discarded. Only then can common good leadership take hold.

Foremost in this undemocratic framework is the belief that corporate leaders are values-neutral. It's a mistake of major proportions to believe that there is anything like values-neutral leadership. The Founding Fathers placed them up front in our Bill of Rights and the Constitution. Because leadership practices – in our country as well as our corporations – are about how people, money and power are managed, they are necessarily an expression of values. Indeed, even talking about a values-neutral approach strikes me as a way to hide basic assumptions that are diametrically opposed to the democratic and humanistic approach in our Constitution. I am gratified that we, at RHD, are open about our values – as well as our effort to walk the walk, and not just talk the talk.

I have met many leaders who assume that employees are essentially lazy and self-interested. This suggests that they need to be directed at every turn – and are somehow worth less than the leaders. Leaders who act on this assumption are rarely required to openly admit it. Unfortunately, this supports an authoritarian abuse of power.

The all-knowing leader is another commonly held belief. I have met many business leaders who assume they know that which is essentially unknowable. Not only do these leaders think they can accurately analyze the past, they talk as though they can predict the future – and therefore have the right to an authoritarian approach to leadership. All-knowing leaders are likely to employ researchers, financial analysts, and statisticians to seek information that supports their particular vision of the future. But how can these tools, that by necessity study the past, generate accurate information about an organization and its market forces in the future? They can't. What they can do is to generate probabilities. They cannot offer the specifics needed for corporate decision-making. Used wisely, such tools can widen a leader's perspective and leave room for group input. This suggests that corporate leaders must limit themselves to making only the most general of decisions while delegating the specifics to staff that is close to the action.

Personal characteristics are highly valued in a leader. I often read business analysts commenting on a leader who has charisma, but rarely do I hear that analyst describe the values that underpin his or her work. Other analysts respect a leader who is pragmatic and action-oriented, but rarely do they try to communicate the basic assumptions about people, power, and money that inform the leader's decisions. Journalists applaud the announcement of a seemingly smart, corporate CEO, the graduate of a prestigious business school whose strategic plan includes new technologies and a carefully designed market research plan, but they are rarely specific about the social behaviors this leader will encourage in the workplace.

It is also likely that commentators do not understand how to surface the values that underpin a leader's approach to money – and whether profit-making will be moderated to permit financial attention to other corporate needs. There are many corporate leaders who believe that those who earn more or sell more are "worth" more. With this approach, financial achievement becomes a reflection of human worth – rather than a consequence of skill, opportunity, and good fortune. It then follows that those who are unsuccessful are worth less, and so deserve less of the material and social goods that corporations can bestow. This financial blind spot can prove fatal to the success of any business and the search for the common good in corporate life.

Given the wide currency of such beliefs, it's no wonder that there is a crisis in corporate leadership in America today: these beliefs are self-serving myths, often unfounded, and ultimately a danger to our country.

It is important to know what a leader believes before we entrust him or her with the power and responsibility of leadership. Values-based leadership is extremely important. This book is filled with descriptions of corporate practices that can only prevail with active and values-based leadership support. They all rely on the conscious use of power.

Leadership practices that I follow.   Underlying the following practices is the belief that my power, and the status that comes with it, is a gift conferred not only by the Board, but importantly, a gift conferred as well by the staff. The gift comes with the responsibility to consciously manage it well.

I watch that my personal preferences do not determine corporate decisions, and that my mood – whether cheerful or irritable – does not affect the corporate atmosphere. Common good leadership requires consciously managing one's personal needs. Only then can I represent, indeed embody, a common good corporate culture.

But when I'm worried, tired, or too intense, I fail to manage my behavior consciously and RHD's values are undermined. When that happens I lose some of the trust that is the basis of my common good power. Fortunately, it is likely that someone will offer me feedback on what went wrong. If I get back on track rapidly, and admit to my limitations, I have found our community to be very forgiving. And so we start down our road again.

Of course as a leader I have the freedom to make decisions based on my own judgment – and sometimes I use that power – but such decisions need to be explained, be open for review, and justified. Furthermore, I suggest that a leader does well to limit his or her use of such power to no more than five percent, and preferably much less, of the time.

I used this power recently when I decided the moment was ripe for the corporation to consider serving the adult imprisoned population. However, to maintain this common-good approach to power, I consciously rejected retaining operational control over the project. Instead of assigning the effort to assistants and asking them for periodic reports, I solicited interest during two open group meetings. And then I called a meeting. Approximately ten people came. The group went through the process of confirming their shared interest, selected a

> Most important is the belief that my power and the status that comes with it is a gift of the Board and staff. And I understand that this gift comes with the responsibility to consciously manage it.

"point person" to manage the effort, and identified others to invite to the next meeting. In so doing it began to have a life of its own. Now my job is to stir up interest among members by encouraging input – and to tolerate the reality that the result of this group effort will be different than would have emerged had I exercised my power to "keep control."

In this example I used my power to lead – and then quickly delegated it. As you have read in the previous chapter, that is one of the practices that maintains a balance between centralization and decentralization.

Delegating power is at the core of my approach to leadership. But true to the search for balance between centralization and decentralization, the thrust toward delegation does not mean that I abdicate the ultimate responsibility for corporate activity – just as the Board maintains ultimate responsibility for my work, I am ultimately responsible for the work of RHD's employees. Just as the Board retains the right of oversight, so do I – along with many others in the corporate office.

It is no secret in RHD that I lead through the delegation of power that is based on trust, mutual respect – and an acceptance of the human possibility for error. When the corporation launches a new project, for instance, I rapidly delegate tasks such as negotiation with our customers, contracts, employment, purchasing, and financial operations. I will offer further input but only if desired. And staff members, who form a new working group, rarely ask for it – perhaps because they want the emotional benefits, including the status and the excitement that comes with shaping a project. I am pleased and consider myself a success when they take such ownership.

This kind of delegation is only possible when I accept the reality that decisions made by others will be different from those that I would make – sometimes better, sometimes worse. Seems obvious but many managers find it very difficult to live with. Often these managers tell me that their job is too big, that it can't be done. Underneath their complaint is, I believe, their difficulty in taking the risks inherent in effective delegation.

Projects fail; problems occur, and money is lost – regardless of our good work. In our RHD culture people are not blamed for these failures as long as their activities

It is no secret in RHD that I lead through the delegation of power that is based on trust, mutual respect – and an acceptance of the human possibility for error.

are not for personal gain, they include the best thinking of others, and they intend to serve the corporation. The absence of blame makes it more likely that the group who made the mistakes will try again – and that's essential to our success.

I recall a time, early in our corporate history, when I first took the risk of delegating an important responsibility. In those beginning days I wrote and negotiated all corporate requests for grants and contracts. Then came the time when I had two assistants who I believed could manage this job with integrity. I knew it was important to delegate the responsibility for this work to them, but I also knew this delegation had to come along with the message that they had my full trust. So with some trepidation, not only did I delegate this corporate power, but after some time I decided not to read the contracts that they wrote – even as I signed them. The message was: "The job and the responsibility are yours. I know you can do it!" We now have literally more than one hundred people exercising this power across the United States.

The results of leadership based on trust can be measured by the growth chart at the beginning of this book and the level of satisfaction at work reached by my fellow employees.

Delegated power is conditional and is withdrawn if the project leader puts the corporation at risk. Experience has led RHD to identify four rules that leaders must follow in order to maintain their power.

Leaders of units or projects are held accountable for the group's fiscal viability. Each project must have a budget that specifies income and expenses, and leaders must adhere to it. If there is evidence of financial difficulty, Central Office staff members intervene, and in extreme cases, take over the leadership.

Clearly, evidence of any illegal activity is cause for immediate intervention. This has very rarely happened in our corporate history.

Endangering corporate relationships with customers is cause for Central Office intervention. We see ourselves as partners with our customers – and staff behaviors that endanger these partnerships need to be quickly challenged.

Leaders who abuse their power are subject to examination. Whether that abuse occurs through authoritarian leadership, actions based on prejudice, preference for certain staff, or inappropriate sexual behavior, the abuse of power is cause for Central Office investigation and possible intervention.

These four rules are very important, but the fact that there are *only* four is even more important.

As a leader my challenge is to listen for the unexpressed and to offer room for frightened people to raise their concern.

Promoting conscious dialogue across the entire staff is essential for the participatory nature of our system. We need a staff that can critically look at their jobs, find trouble spots, and advocate for change. We need open debate because we know that it goes a long way toward solving corporate problems.

To support a dialogue in meetings, I generally avoid a pre-set agenda – thus making it likely that staff will introduce items of interest to them. However, some people are critical of this approach; I have heard it said that meetings in RHD are too chaotic, too free-floating, that there are too many items being considered, too many people having a say. Certainly not everyone is comfortable with the messy, rather untidy way such open-ended meetings work. But often the energy is almost palpable and the outcome exciting.

This open-ended form of meeting cannot thrive without a safe and open environment. For this reason we use facilitators to help groups create this safety. Sometimes these group process meetings are difficult for me. Indeed, in the midst of one I often find myself sitting back in my chair and taking a deep breath. They take patience and time.

Especially when nothing seems to be happening, a leader needs the determined strength, good humor, and often the help of a facilitator, to patiently listen for the unexpressed and to offer room for people to raise their concern. And when the first signs of staff creativity emerge, to respond with support and interest.

Too many corporations ignore the opinions of their line staff – and rely on leaders to communicate top-down information to staff. Here's an e-mail example from an RHD staff member who moved on to a job in another corporation:

> *My predecessor, who is now my boss, is often non-communicative and seems to have a tough time relating to others in the corporation. As a result, there is a very high turnover rate and low staff morale in the office. Strategic planning meetings have been set up to focus on*

communication. And a global staff satisfaction survey indicates that the top issue is a lack of communication. It is amazing to me that executive management has had a really tough time understanding what the lack of communication might mean. One of the first solutions proposed in a recent meeting (by my boss) was to form more committees. The LAST thing people want to do is go to more meetings. Meetings here consist of sitting in a chair while someone talks at you.

– Sandy

It's all too easy for leaders to inhibit the participation of employees – especially those who do not have the verbal skills to object appropriately, or are in desperate need of the job. After many years in abusive workplaces, others are simply too frightened to speak

In the course of a workday most RHD leaders know they are ordinary human beings and so do not have all the answers. They understand that employees close to the action can suggest creative solutions to corporate problems. They are able to talk about mistakes that they make, judgments that do not work out, and business efforts that lose money. I model this behavior to communicate that I, too, am a bumbling fool who is simply trying to find his way through the next day. After all, I never ran a $162,000,000 corporation before.

Ideas-In-Practice

To conclude this chapter on common good leadership, I offer a brief history of the praxis – ideas-in-practice – that underpins the thirty-seven years of RHD's development.

But first, an old question: Which came first the chicken or the egg? Did I create the corporation or did the corporation create me as a leader? Clearly, the question has no simple answer. At every stage of corporate development, the chicken had an effect on the next egg and the egg had an effect on the evolving chicken. Out of the interaction, both the corporation and I emerged.

As an example, I was reading about the current estrangement of Muslims in the Western world, and suggested to Barbara that it was time to start a discussion group that would offer Muslim staff a chance to participate as Muslims in the corporate community. I thought of a name for the group – Muslim Voices in RHD – and suggested a staff person to lead the effort. Barbara responded with the name of another person, someone with more maturity and more experience in the corporation. This suggestion gave a different shape to the project, and later in the day, when this woman agreed to join with me, I knew she would further shape the effort. How strange that people should think of leadership as a solo practice.

In 1969, after having worked in several hospitals, a family service agency, and a university, I approached the challenge of creating a new community mental health center with the intention to widen the scope of the organization as quickly as possible. I believed that RHD had to develop into a multi-purpose organization to be a successful and sustainable social tool.

The single purpose social agencies I had experienced did not have the flexibility to address the multiple problems people face when trying to improve their lives. Secondly, I knew that the single purpose organization was dependent on a single funding stream. And given that particular human services can lose their governmental support while other trendier services attract dollars, a single purpose funding stream can become a trickle rather than a flow.

In those early days I was interested in the diversified corporate holding company – a business model that was spreading across the private sector in the late 1960s. With a centralized financial and marketing system, these holding companies contained many subsidiary corporations that produced a range of products. For example, an integrated diversified corporate holding company could grow food and then process, package, market, and truck it. That same company could also own the store that sold it. The holding company was a powerhouse of possibilities.

While these for-profit efforts were mushrooming across the country, the non-profit sector was still struggling to launch and maintain single purpose efforts – perhaps a family counseling agency, probably in a poor community, with limited funding from a local government agency.

The difference between the two models troubled me. I did not want to spend much of my time seeking donations to keep such an organization alive, and I knew that depending on private donations from wealthy people demanded more energy than I could give. Still I wanted to build a powerful corporate tool that would address social issues. Perhaps, I thought, the holding company would offer a better way.

Not that the for-profit holding company model worked well all the time. In fact, mergers led to many failures – and still do. When large for-profits bought and then integrated smaller companies they often found that market share, innovation, and creativity dropped, and anger at the parent company rose. Indeed, because of this phenomenon, many business people gave up on the diversified holding company.

That reaction was unfortunate. I knew there was a better way to manage a holding company, but to make that happen leaders would have to give up on the tried and true – in effect, they would have to give up on centralizing their approach to managing people, power, and money.

I believed the holding company model could work at RHD if we decentralized decision-making in general, and most important, decentralized day-to-day monetary decisions. My values led me to think that there were many ways to seek corporate success – and diversity was therefore a valuable tool.

This new model would spread decision-making across working groups – each with its separate corporate culture – while the parent company would centralize program oversight and financial strength. Those who were building the corporation with me joined in this direction. It was a risk; we did not know how well it could be done, but slowly we did it.

For the first few years the counseling center and the corporate leaders shared a common space. But as soon as RHD assumed responsibility for a second unit – a methadone center – the Central Office was formed and its personnel were moved into a separate space. In this way we established a parent company and two self-directed units, each of which had a separate budget and its own personnel. In the late seventies we established a series of other programs, and true to the holding company model, each became a separate unit with its own space, name, and budget. In this way our structure was established.

From RHD's inception I also put energy into developing a values-based interpersonal culture. As a family therapist, I understood how destructive hostile conflicts were to family systems. And I opposed tolerating such behaviors in our new corporate experiment. Happily, virtually everyone I spoke to agreed with me. However, no one had an explicit strategy for implementing this healthier approach. There were no written materials that clarified how leadership could maintain the ultimate authority over money and power, while not tolerating an excess of authoritarian right/wrong thinking in our work environments.

...no one, including me, had the "right" answer.

Over the years we figured out how to do it. Perhaps it happened because we accepted the reality that no one, including me, had the "right" answer to specific corporate problems. Maybe it happened because we created a culture that balanced respect for the leader without encouraging dependence on him or her for ultimate answers. And there was no doubt: I wanted to be questioned – it stimulated me to re-think positions and include the concerns raised by others. Past "solutions" were always up for revision. Our decision-making came in a group process form that included introducing a possible solution, revising it, seeking further input, and then revising again. This process has become an important part of RHD's corporate culture. It also helped us to be wary of anyone who offers absolute answers.

I still observe that I'm an "absolute relativist" – under any and all circumstances, I believe that there are a number of workable answers to any corporate problem.

As RHD moved into the 1980s and '90s the number of units became ten, twenty and more, each with its own identity. Soon I realized that I had to provide an organized voice for all the units. It was understandable, indeed I would say necessary, that there would be a push and pull between the center and the units, and we had to create a structure that would allow both sides to be heard. This led to the formation of the Unit Directors Group. I knew that the tension would remain – and that it was good. If we stayed open to that conflict we would be able to figure out where centralization was necessary and where decentralization was possible – and why. It would give us room for the expression of resistance – a place in which authority could be questioned rather than blindly followed.

About twenty years ago RHD began to generate sufficient discretionary money to engage in common good activities beyond those that government was able to support. And so we created new research and development efforts. Endow A Home, for instance, is a unit funded by private donors that offers homeless mothers and their children a chance to choose a home selling at $38,000, which they can buy back when they are able – at the same price. Another effort, called New Beginnings, is a non-profit incubator for social entrepreneurs. To help them establish themselves, groups with a social purpose are offered desk space, office tools, and business consultation. In this way a children's museum, various arts programs and a medical fund for women in need began. Many other such research and development efforts are ongoing.

About fifteen years ago RHD moved into the for-profit world and so formed Murex, Inc. as a for-profit subsidiary. With this corporate tool in hand we could enter into for-profit, socially-oriented activities. Our efforts included a woman-led computer repair company and a woman-led construction company. Urban Works, an industrial cleaning company, was still another; currently it employs eighty workers, providing salaries, benefits and the possibility of participation in profits.

Most important, this for-profit activity offers us an opportunity to demonstrate an economic model that addresses the growing economic inequality across our society: workers participate in upside of the business; namely, in profit when it is available. A portion of the profit is allocated to address social issues; in fact, I recently received a $17,000 check earmarked for that purpose as a donation to the non-profit parent company from one of our for-profit businesses. In this case, the social sector was included in the deal – a percentage of profits that was defined in the partners' agreement must be donated to a non-profit. Our newest business, a pharmacy, will distribute a majority of its profits to fund health care for the medically indigent.

I look forward to the further growth of RHD as a tool for social change. We are big enough now to bring together synergistic teams of people that reflect the wide range of experience in RHD. In themselves, these teams are the tools that are needed for an innovative approach to social issues.

And as the corporation expands there will be significant increases in the amount of discretionary funds available to support such non-profit activities as well as to invest in socially innovative for-profit businesses.

Please visit www.common goodcorporation. org to join with us in this effort.

I look forward to the further growth of RHD as a tool for social change.

RHD is a demonstration of the viability of a Common Good Corporation and as such, I believe, it will help others involved in similar efforts. I hope that others will copy some of our practices, improve on others and teach us about what they are involved in. There is room for numerous Common Good Corporations in the for-profit and non-profit arenas. Please visit www.commongoodcorporation.org to join with us in this effort. I believe that together we can find our way.

I like the story of the person who is lost and seeing a local farmer, asks for directions. This farmer says, "You can't get there from here – but there's a place down this road, about a mile, and I can tell you how to get there from there." I am often confused about how to make things happen but if I ask others to join me, one of them is likely to point us in the right direction.

CHAPTER VII

SEX IN THE OFFICE

I was having lunch with a colleague from another corporation when the topic of sex in the office came up. And the man bristled: "As far as I'm concerned sex has no place in the office. It causes too much trouble. In fact my corporation has a policy that doesn't allow for any intimate relationships. When it surfaces one of the troublemakers has to leave."

This man's position is common in the corporate world. Sexual issues, often uncomfortable to deal with, lead many managers to ignore them until absolutely necessary. To make matters worse, there is also an almost total absence of professional writing on the topic. All this avoidance leads to sex becoming the proverbial elephant sitting in the middle of an office while no one acknowledges its existence – even though it's a major topic of interest, and might, at times, take up more employee time than the development of a new product or sales strategy.

However, including a chapter on sex in the office is not simply to encourage efficiency. It is an illustration of how to breathe life into common good principles. In the last two chapters we have considered how a corporation can be used to move toward equalizing the power of employees; namely, through a decentralized structure and/or through non-authoritarian leadership. Now we can see how this values-based effort to equalize power works when applied to sexual behaviors that occur in the office.

Broadly defined, sex in the office can include relationships that culminate in marriage, much flirting, and many different kinds of affairs. It also includes the use of computers for sex-related personal communications with other adults. Then there are all the abusive behaviors of those who mix power with sex as they harass, stalk, or force contact with adults as well as activities that are illegal. My view is that all these activities need management oversight – but with different kinds of managerial interventions.

Courtships, engagements, and marriage

Perhaps easiest of all interventions for managers, is to celebrate a sexual relationship that leads to marriage:

Picture fifty people standing in the dark waiting. Someone, it is unclear who, takes on the authoritative role of "shushing" the group when voices begin to grow loud. The room is hot, people are a little uncomfortable but they stand still quietly. Finally the door opens framing Barry and Jen – who look a little confused and then shocked as the lights go on, plastic wine glasses are raised, and everyone screams, "Surprise!"

Barry and Jen are being celebrated. They just got married. And everyone is happy.

Standing there in the dark a couple of people, including the manager who arranged for the celebration, recalled celebrating seven other RHD Central Office employee marriages. There had to be many others that took place in the units.

Here celebration is a tool that can be used to build workplace communities, and in so doing, to foster qualities such as loyalty, creativity, and a sense of well-being. Managers in RHD do well to take advantage of opportunities to create such events.

Then there are other office wide sexual issues that arise and require still other, perhaps not so easy forms of intervention. And sometimes there is the choice to not intervene.

The dress code issue

It's springtime as I write this, and with over 185 employees in the corporate office alone, I'm aware that the issue of "appropriate dress" (read "too sloppy or sexually explicit") will come up very soon. I also know that it's a chance to further our approach to corporate management by applying our assumptions and

...a chapter on managing sexual behaviors in the office is not simply to encourage efficiency. It's an illustration of how to breathe life into common good principles.

our values – the assumption that there is no one right way to deal with corporate issues is certainly relevant in this case.

Most corporate leaders act as though they have the responsibility, the intelligence, and the particular expertise to know what is right – including what is the "right" way to dress in the office. Yet when I talk privately with one of these leaders, perhaps over a drink, I'm likely to hear, "Damn if I know what to do in this situation. That's beyond me!"

Yet they often return to their offices and slip into the myth of the all-knowing leader. Perhaps this is because the role of the one who "knows" and the one who has power are joined in the larger culture. These are the leaders who mandate a dress code for an entire corporation. It's an authoritarian approach – and therefore runs counter to RHD's value that leaders cannot use their authority to impose their personal views.

While many corporate leaders think that dress codes and corporate productivity are directly related, I actually think the opposite is true. Instead, the absence of a dress code is a way to encourage creativity – it comes with a willingness to think out-of-the-box and a curiosity about the new and the different.

Sometimes, however, employees go too far – by that I mean their dress is obviously sexual and beyond the tolerance of many people in their small group. Since authority is decentralized in RHD, unless corporate involvement is necessary, we ask small groups to do the work of openly discussing and influencing dress code decisions.

This means that although, as a leader, I want RHD's employees to dress freely, it must be in a way that their small groups think appropriate. I model this in my own behavior – people know when I'm going to see a banker or a government official because I dress in a way I think is appropriate to the situation – with a jacket and a tie. Otherwise, I dress casually.

While small groups in RHD are responsible for their own dress norms, I'm also aware that many small group managers avoid facing such issues, which suggests that opportunities for supervision are being missed. The following set of e-mails between a corporate office manager and me illustrates this issue.

Dear Bob.

In my last job I had to wear a suit – and I hated it. So, when I came for an interview at RHD and saw how casually, but neatly, people dressed, I was impressed. There were many reasons that led me to take the job, but I particularly liked that. However, I believe that my staff goes too far. If you could see Joan, you would know what I mean. Yesterday she wore a pair of slim hip-hugging jeans and a form-fitting top that had a considerable cleavage. Throughout the entire day a stream of young men managed to find the time to stop by and visit her. And you should hear the comments people made; one employee said, 'It's a wonder that all these guys have time to work.' Joan is a good worker but I'm sorely tempted to ask her to dress more professionally. I wonder why we don't have a dress code.

And I wrote back:

I suggest that you raise the issue of dress in a staff meeting of your department – and please set aside your personal views so that you can surface and show respect for the view of others. In this way you avoid acting alone as a manager, and demonstrate a decision-making process in which your views are not the only ones to be followed. If the group agrees that some standards need to be set ask them to clarify those standards. Then be clear about who will talk to a member if his or her dress is out of line with others in the group – and try not to be the person to lead this process. If this meeting doesn't resolve the dress code issue, include your supervisor in the next meeting – and try again.

Although this approach is not intended to stop you from making a decision, it is intended to encourage you and all leaders not to be overbearing or to let your opinion rule the day. In this way we intentionally make it difficult for an authoritarian leader to find a home in RHD.

Office flirtations

Create a group, and eventually the pull of sexual attraction will arise within it. We all know the ritual; one human being approaches another with a charged sexual energy, and the other responds or doesn't. If he or she does, the coupling dance begins. And it's rarely a secret. I have seen flirtations generate a vibrancy, keen attention and what might be called a positive irreverence – all qualities that, hopefully, can carry over into corporate work. And there are times when a flirtation notches up the energy in a workgroup.

However, many colleagues wonder to themselves or out loud: Are they dating? Are they suited for each other? Are they ready for it? Will he or she treat the other badly or lovingly? Flirtations are also a prime ground for judgment. Some disapprove of gay relationships, others of interracial attachments, and still others disapprove of any relationship if it takes place at work. All this changes across time. Not too many years ago those over sixty were thought too old to flirt.

In RHD most often we consciously manage sexual behaviors with a hands-off approach. For instance most flirtations in the office are not suppressed primarily because our values lead us toward respecting individual freedom. Also we have seen that this kind of sexuality can generate vibrancy, a curiosity and positive irreverence – qualities that hopefully are integrated into corporate work.

However, there are employees who don't know how to relate to their colleagues except through flirtations. That requires supervision – the kind that can coach such employees on how to de-sexualize their workplace behavior.

Recently I participated in dispelling blame when Joan, a colleague, stopped by my desk with a glint in her eye and said, "I just passed the mail room and noticed George and Madeline in a very private tête-à-tête – looks like something is going on."

Joan assumed that I would be interested in this information – and in this case I was, somewhat. George is an important member of the corporation and what people think of him is important. He needs the good will of others to do his job. I remembered how upset the office was when he left his wife last year – she also worked in the Central Office, and many people felt loyal to her. At the time I tried to affect this judgment by commenting on how important it is that we have the freedom to make personal choices in our country and in our workplace. So I was interested in what Joan had to say about this new office buzz.

She continued, "Now that his ex-wife has resigned, the office is following this new relationship happily. Looks like they have forgiven him."

I felt pleased about this – not only for George but also for the corporation. The talk about which sexual behaviors are right and which are wrong leads to blame and considerable shame in those who are being sexual. This problem is not solely related to sex; it affects the readiness with which people are able to quickly move to blaming others when it comes to other corporate issues.

Then there are the even more difficult situations that managers must face, times when they must intervene.

The problem of overlapping roles

Sometimes the sexual dance occurs between employees of different corporate status, with one partner having supervisory power over another. This becomes a corporate issue because an administrative relationship and a personal relationship are joined together – with one person having more corporate power than the other. Such power differentials, with their potential for abuse, are exactly what we strive to undo in the corporation. If, however, that differential does not exist, and both people want the sexual relationship, there is no reason at RHD for a manager to do anything.

When a corporate power differential is present our policy states that the couple must immediately inform the two corporate managers responsible for oversight of this policy – the CEO and his or her management partner. Then the supervisory role must be shifted to another person, making it less likely that the sexual issues will be used to further or interfere with one person's career. This policy has been used numerous times. Many of these relationships have ended. A few have resulted in marriage.

A Hub manager told me the following story:

> *Mercedes and John became lovers while working in an RHD unit. She was a Unit Director and he was a supervisor. He was answerable to her. Trouble was, even though John knew a lot about his job, he often confronted angrily and some people were afraid of him. No one in the unit spoke about the problem – until the unit had financial issues and layoffs were imminent. Then it exploded – in an open meeting when a Citizen Advocate announced, "Staff are grumbling about John; they're sure he won't get laid off because of his relationship with Mercedes."*

...experience has taught me that a working group that avoids authoritarian and/or simplistic blame is happier and more productive.

John's supervision was shifted to another person and a note was added to Mercedes' personnel record. She was criticized for not reporting the personal relationship earlier so that John's supervision could be changed to another person. After another three months he was asked to leave due to his volatile behavior.

Sometimes it takes a crisis for a problem to surface, and when it does, there is another opportunity to apply corporate values.

Sexual harassment

Unfortunately, some people force their sexual attention on others – in so doing they destroy the safe and open environments our small groups need to function. Indeed, creating and sustaining these safe and open environments is essential for our decentralized structure.

Shelly complained to her co-workers that Joe was staring at her, following her when she walked to her bus stop. "It felt creepy!" Shortly after these conversations her remarks reached the ears of an Associate Director of the corporation. As it turned out, this Director's job included assuring that women in the office felt safe. In this capacity she asked Shelly about Joe. And then, with Shelly's story in hand, she followed policy.

The policy indicates that a sexual harassment complaint must be brought to the attention of me, the CEO. And since I'm male, it also stipulates that a female Associate Director be included in reviewing and managing the situation. During the ensuing investigation the Associate Director and I listened to Joe explain his behavior. He argued that there was no problem in what he did: "Shelly's attractive and I like to look at her. So several times a day I went out of my way to pass her desk. Nothing wrong about looking at an attractive woman."

I tried to explain to Joe that when one of our employees doesn't want his attention, my job, and the job of the corporation, is to protect and respect her privacy. But Joe wasn't convinced. Indeed, nothing changed during the next few weeks. Finally, my colleague and I presented him with a simple alternative – either avoid the area around Shelly's desk, or after the next episode, I would personally fire him. He stopped harassing Shelly. That was 15 years ago. The problem has not surfaced again.

A Common Good Corporation needs policies to manage harassment and the overlap of personal and professional roles in work relationships. Most important, when these troublesome behaviors are not present, it is essential to avoid negatively judging any of the endless varieties of human sexual behavior – and to keep sex in the office open for discussion. The more open an environment the more likely the rumors that are usually underground will surface – and so give management the opportunity to respond. This is particularly important when one or another employee thinks that a corporate action, or lack of action, is unfair. This, too, is an opportunity to teach the values.

Here's a story that illustrates the complexity of a sexual event that took place in an RHD office. Human knowledge is very unstable; we know almost everything we know incompletely. And what seems obvious turned out to be false.

> It is essential to avoid negatively judging any of the endless varieties of human sexual behavior – and to keep sex in the office open for discussion.

CAROL AND ELIZABETH

Word came back to the Central Office that an office employee named Carol, who worked in an outpatient setting, had a picture of a penis on her computer. Apparently she and other employees were standing around the computer laughing at the image when Elizabeth, one of the clinical staff, walked by. She felt threatened by the image and believed it was unprofessional to show it at work. Elizabeth expressed her chagrin to a government official that happened to be visiting the unit – before bringing her concern to the attention of her supervisor or her small group.

Because our relationship with this government contractor was at stake, people in the Central Office felt it necessary to intervene. Recall, threatening customer relationships has always been one of the very few reasons for which we move toward a centralized response (see Chapter V).

And so two Central Office managers visited the unit to investigate the accusation. But they couldn't find any evidence of pornographic material on the computer. When they spoke to Carol she denied the accusation. Meanwhile several other unit staff expressed their annoyance at the corporation's intrusion into their work place.

The Central Office managers were baffled. However, given the RHD policy that prohibits the use of corporate computers for sexual material, they thought they were right to intervene. Trouble is, they forgot that the policy prohibits only the use of computers for illegal activity.

Knowing the tendency in our American culture to clamp down on sexual behaviors even if they are not harmful or illegal, when I was informed of this Central Office activity I chose to intervene. It was one of those situations that I believed could be managed so as to once again model our basic assumptions.

Given further investigation, a very different picture emerged. It seems that it was a group of female employees who were laughing as they stood around Carol's computer. And Elizabeth, who was passing by, chose to see what they were laughing about. As it turned out, as a professional, Elizabeth already felt this group was exhibiting behaviors that should not be tolerated in an office. The computer event tipped the scale for her. In her mind, Carol's behavior was outrageous. She therefore mentioned it to the outside official

Here's what I determined: Since all of the people involved were female; there was no sexual material being introduced that might be considered harassment by a male. Furthermore, since Elizabeth chose to approach the group to look at the computer, she wasn't being harassed. And lastly, because there was already tension between Elizabeth and others in the office staff, this was a local administrative problem.

Most important for the maintenance of a safe and open environment, although Elizabeth could have confronted the other women involved directly, or requested a small group meeting, she did neither. Instead, she used the incident to attack a work group that she disliked. All this led me, and the small group working with me, to conclude that corporate intrusion into the unit was taken too soon – before the full picture was discovered, discussed and clarified. As a result we requested that the Unit Director discuss this staff relations problem with her staff and I apologized for the intrusion of staff from the Central Office.

This wasn't the first time in RHD's history that sexual issues were used to heighten an already existing conflict between people. Claims of harassment are often raised after a person is terminated or confronted on a poor job performance. Although every claim must be rapidly evaluated, accusations of inappropriate sexuality can be made for reasons other than employee harassment.

This story is interesting to me as a manager because it addresses several major values-based quandaries that arise in the management of people. The RHD assumption that every employee is of equal human worth leads to the value of respect for each individual. We therefore respect the privacy of people and keep out of their sexual lives, if behaviors are not illegal and/or do not interfere with our maintenance of another value – the corporate effort to create safe and open environments. Honoring both these values is of keen importance to all of us when it comes to managing people.

Finally, our decentralized structure distributes corporate power by empowering small working groups to manage their own issues. To accomplish this we must maintain the boundary between those small groups and the Central Office, thereby avoiding centralized control whenever possible.

CHAPTER VIII

MONEY: PART ONE

Money...money... money...money... If ever there was a culture obsessed with money, it is ours. Most of us work for it, dream about it, and some even steal for it. Certainly the corporate leaders who have gotten caught stealing for money, pay a big price. But, for most of us, this does not diminish the obsession to get it – as well as the power and status it brings. So the subject of money has an important place in a book about the Common Good Corporation.

Let's begin with the basics: Money is a tool created by people, and like any tool, including the corporation itself, it can be used either poorly or well dependent on the values of the people who use it.

The money tool is used to exchange the work of people and the things they make for the work of other people and the things they make. In modern times, however, money comes with a mutation: interest is added to it, and this profoundly changes the nature of the exchange. Indeed, the American dollar is called an interest-bearing currency. To understand how interest plays a part in an exchange, we must take a look at the Federal Banking System (the Fed).

Later in this chapter and those which follow we'll compare our interest-bearing dollar to an alternative currency suggested by Silvio Gesell,[1] a 19th century German sociologist who was concerned about the implications of an interest-bearing currency. I offer Gesell's model not as an alternative to ours, but as a stimulus that will help us to recognize that the money tool does not have to come

---

[1] Gesell, Silvio. 1909. *The Natural Economic Order.* Great Britain: Peter Owen, LTD.

in its current form. Finally, we'll turn to RHD to see how money is created in the organization and used to operate a Common Good Corporation.

THE FEDERAL RESERVE BANKING SYSTEM (THE FED)

The Fed is the nation's central bank. Created by an Act of Congress in 1913, it provides the commercial banking system with currency and commercial paper, and controls the amount of money available.

The Fed consists of a seven-member Board of Governors and twelve Reserve Banks located in major cities throughout the United States. The Board of Governors is appointed by the President and confirmed by the Senate to serve 14-year terms of office. Presidents Reagan, Bush, Clinton, and Bush all selected Alan Greenspan as the Chairman of the Board, and he served in this capacity through 2005. Currently, Ben S. Bernanke holds the position.

Here's a simple version of how this financial system works: Periodically the Fed does the necessary economic research, and in agreement with the U.S. Treasury, issues a certain amount of credit and authorizes the production of a certain amount of bills and coins. For our purposes, I'll refer to all these products as currency.

The Fed makes this money available to the twelve member banks at no cost. In turn, these member banks make this currency, plus an interest rate, available to their most prominent and stable business customers; namely large banks and other financial institutions. These large banks and institutions lend to smaller banks and financial institutions at higher interest rates. Then these smaller banks lend at a still higher rate to the vast array of smaller corporations and other forms of small businesses. As you can see, it is through an interest-bearing centralized currency that each level of our nation's financial system makes money.

The Federal Reserve Board of Governors also has the responsibility for deciding on and regulating monetary policy. With an eye on promoting national economic goals, it takes actions that influence both the availability and the cost of money.

Federal Reserve Banks generate income to cover their own expenses, primarily from the interest they earn on government securities. They are not, however, operated for a profit. Each year they return to the U.S. Treasury all earnings in excess of Federal Reserve operating expenses.

Let's turn to an individual consumer to further understand the role of interest in our economy. Clearly by the time a consumer goes into a store to buy a washing machine, the money this consumer pays must cover the interest charged by multiple layers of our fiscal system – the manufacturer of the washing machine has probably borrowed money at interest, perhaps from a bank, which borrowed it from a larger bank.

Perhaps this manufacturer also bought raw materials from one corporation and legal services from another – in each case the price included the cost of interest on the money borrowed. Therefore, to make a profit, the manufacturer of the washing machine has to pass on to the consumer the cost for all of this interest.

In this way the banking system and these multiple businesses are supported by what he or she pays for the machine. However, this consumer is likely not to be aware of it. And if asked, might very well respond, "Well, that's the way the system works."

It's true, that's the way the system works. And it works well, fairly well, but only if a person or a company has excess money. In our financial system only those who have excess money can make more money by saving or lending it at interest, or investing it for profit, and still have money left for their daily needs. Others who earn their money in the form of a salary tend to spend most of it on essentials such as housing and food. They do not earn enough to make money on money. So they never get ahead, and in today's economy, most are falling behind. That's also how the system works. I do believe that there's something essentially wrong with a system that penalizes people who can only sell their time – or the goods and services they personally produce. Why should those people be at a disadvantage?

If the goal is to create an increasing separation between the haves and the have-nots, the interest-bearing centralized system that produces the U.S. dollar is phenomenally effective. Those who have excess money continually increase

> ...to make a profit the manufacturer of a washing machine has to pass on to the consumer the cost for all of this interest – this consumer is likely not to be aware of it.

their wealth by charging interest. They are ahead of the game. In fact the Financial Times reported that only 2% of the world's population now own 50% of the world's assets.[2]

And consumers, most of whom are middle class or the working poor, foot the bill – through the interest they pay each time they make a purchase. With salaries that remain fairly stable, and without saved money that can be used to make interest, they have to lose the game. And, by the way, the Fed never issues money to pay the interest that accumulates on loaned principal, and therefore the supply is always insufficient to cover accumulated interest. That means that some people certainly must lose at this game – and give up their car, home, farm or business investment.

If we truly believed in the assumption of equal human worth, and we wanted our financial markets to reflect that value, we would adjust the functions of the central bank to create more level playing fields for certain economic functions such as the construction of schools. As it is, the financially successful can believe that they are inherently better than others, smart enough to be born into money or able to use their wits to make it, lend it, or invest it. The Federal Banking System supports that distortion given the absence of a level playing field. But we don't have to live that distortion in a Common Good Corporation

Common good values emphasize equal human worth, freedom, and economically healthy communities. Our current monetary system leads those who have money to believe that equalizing efforts are not in their self-interest. Because public education, health, and community improvement are paid for with tax dollars, they are resisted or ignored. That leads to the increased separation between the haves and have-nots and contributes to the resultant social breakdown. Often, those who accumulate excess money from this interest-bearing money system think that their wealth can buy them the power to avoid the results of such social breakdown.

I offer Gessell's model not as an alternative to ours, but as a stimulus that might allow us to let go of the notion that money can only come in its current form.

---

[2] The Financial Times. Chris Giles. *Half the world's assets held by 2% of population.* December 8, 2006

COMPANION CURRENCIES

It's important to keep in mind that nation states create their currencies, and therefore, can create alternative and/or companion currencies that would work according to different rules. The currency we will look at now is more likely to permit common good values in corporate and/or personal situations.

In his book *The Natural Economic Order*, Silvio Gesell who was born in 1862, suggested what he called "a companion currency." This currency does not allow people to earn interest on money.

Gesell also talked about money as nothing more than a tool – an "indispensable manufactured article." He observed that "good money" is an efficient instrument of exchange, and if well made, will work for everyone in a society. On the other hand, he added, most currencies are inefficient or "bad money."

To correct this problem, he suggested that nations use two forms of currency: one for goods that require time to develop value (for example, capital goods such as buildings and machinery). The other is a "companion" currency, used for buying perishable goods and labor, both of which actually have a time-bound value. For example, the laborer's work lasts no longer than the period of time it is sold for, and a perishable food quickly becomes inedible. Instead of developing value, they lose value over time.

The current American dollar is used to pay for capital goods such as buildings and machinery as well as to purchase worker time and perishable goods. And since the dollar always bears interest, it provides the owners with an unfair advantage. They can hold on to their interest-bearing money while gaining interest until the time is ripe for a good investment. Those who are trying to sell their perishable goods or labor can't hold out until the price for their goods is higher.

In contrast, Gesell suggests that the American type of currency be used only to purchase capital goods, and an interest-free companion currency be introduced, which would be used to purchase worker time and perishable goods.

Just as worker time and perishable goods lose value over time, so would this interest-free currency lose value over time in a process called demurrage. Of

> Gesell also talked about money as nothing more than a tool – an "indispensable manufactured article."

importance, the companion currency would not compete with the American dollar because it could not be used to buy capital items.

As defined, this companion money would be spent rapidly because it could not be usefully saved, loaned at interest or used for long-term investments. Therefore the worker who sells his time and the producer who sells perishable goods would find eager buyers.

We would still have the standard interest-bearing currency, the dollar, as we know it, to save, loan and invest in capital goods like houses, factories, machinery and cars. In effect, the interest-bearing currency would be used to create wealth – but would not deny people adequate pay for their work or food for their families.

Perceptively, Gesell predicted that if Western industrialized countries continued to solely depend on interest-bearing currencies to sustain their economies, they would be plagued by the very social problems our world is currently facing.

Of most importance, however, is Gesell's insight that money is simply a tool – and if the tool we are using contributes to social and economic problems – we can consider introducing changes or developing new tools.

There are contemporary alternatives to the interest-bearing dollar. One doesn't necessarily have to use money to make a profit or produce a high interest to produce the maximum gain. Excess or discretionary money can, and is, routinely used to support loved ones – spouses, children and perhaps siblings and parents. Others give it to their communities or to friends. Still others lend it at no interest to friends as an expression of caring particularly because it is without interest.

There are those who give money to individuals or groups for whom the federal government doesn't allow a tax write-off. In so doing, they consciously disregard the tax implications that might transform their donations into some financial benefit. And there are local community movements such as babysitting exchanges or food and purchasing co-ops in which members donate their time without pay, and keep track of that time as a measurement of exchange.

In other words, people can and do use money, or a portion of their money, outside the interest-bearing, business-oriented, personal gain system. This allows them to address diverse social goals. However, since they only have interest-bearing money as a paradigm, they tend to give it sparingly, particularly when giving to others outside the family or supporting community needs. What a different world it would be if we found ourselves with too much companion currency for our personal needs.

Once we free ourselves from the assumption that we must increase our money as fast and as much as possible, we can discover the many ways it can be used creatively to address common good goals in the modern corporation. RHD is proving it every single day. And one of the remarkable effects is a rapidly growing, financially robust corporation.

CORPORATE OPERATIONAL SPENDING

Operational spending is defined, for this purpose, as those funds used to maintain the year-to-year operations of a corporation. My goal is to stimulate consideration of a values-based approach to this spending – and to emphasize that whatever the approach, it either supports or undercuts stated values in the rest of corporate life.

The first step is to initiate an honest debate about traditional corporate financial thinking versus common good financial thinking, to include as many stakeholders as possible, and to explore alternative approaches to the way monetary decisions are made – and who makes them.

Each corporation needs a set of common good fiscal policies. What has worked at RHD will obviously be different from what works in another corporation. However, as you read about the fiscal actions that RHD has taken and the reasons for them, you may conceive of actions that better apply to your corporation. In essence, the search is for a third way – neither traditional fiscal management nor RHD's approach, but some rendition of a both/and solution.

Here is a list of the shifts in thinking that I believe are needed to affect traditional fiscal management to create an individually designed, common good approach to corporate fiscal management.

> Once we free ourselves from the assumption that we must increase our money as fast and as much as possible, we can discover many ways it can be used to address common good goals in the modern corporation.

Most corporate managers believe that fiscal decisions must be centralized to achieve the most efficient use of money to satisfy obligations and produce profits. Alternatively, Common Good managers shape a centralized fiscal policy, which addresses these obligations, and also identifies how decisions will be made, and who will make them, when profits are produced. If workers and line managers are committed to making a profit they will find ways to do so. In order to get their commitment, they need a voice in how profits will be used. RHD has found that when a considerable portion of profits, or discretionary funds, are used to enhance the lives of workers and the community, that commitment is maximized. There needs to be a decision-making process regarding that money. Obviously, to achieve this the amount of funds that are centralized must be limited so that each group can work toward a successful financial goal.

Most corporate managers believe that money must be used to enhance the status and power of key managers. Alternatively, Common Good managers understand that corporate prosperity is likely to multiply if local managers are also provided with the status and the power necessary to make appropriate local fiscal decisions.

Most corporate managers believe that employees cannot be trusted to use money to further the corporation's best interests. Alternatively, although centralized oversight is necessary, local fiscal managers can be taught to establish and follow budgets that meet financial goals for corporate as well as local financial gain. The RHD experiment proves that these two goals are intimately connected.

RHD's Operational Expenses

Let's now turn to RHD and see how operational money is used in this Common Good Corporation. Succinctly said, as much as possible, we use the money tool to give life to our equal human worth value, and so reduce the distance between the haves and have-nots. Once again, I need to say that our fiscal path is not necessarily the "right" one. Out of context, there is no "right" one. Only corporate leaders steeped in a corporation's operations can shape financial policy.

During the 2004-05 fiscal year, RHD's non-profit revenues, primarily from government, but also from foundation, corporate and individual grants, totaled $108,680,000. Of this, 91% was used for operational expenditures. This chapter is about the values-based financial decisions RHD makes to manage the 91%. The remaining 9% constitute what I call discretionary money, which will be discussed in the next chapter.

Given how big a slice of the pie our operational expenditures take, decisions about managing this slice are bound to have a profound effect on our culture and the methods we use to equalize human worth.

Open communication

First and foremost, common good financial goals are approached through open communication (See chapter IV.) The respect and trust that comes with honest communication about money allows staff at all levels to emotionally invest in the corporation. On the other hand continued silence about money, compensation and monetary policy breeds distrust and alienation between those in power and those who actually operate the corporation. I believe that open communication can lead to a rich array of ideas and practices – and the energy that increases corporate effectiveness.

As I write this chapter RHD is still dealing with the effects that Hurricane Katrina had on over one hundred staff, consumers and relatives living in or around New Orleans. During an RHD Council meeting held shortly after the hurricane hit, a number of line staff in the Philadelphia area asked what the corporation was doing to help staff affected by the hurricane. Their interest and the ensuing discussion stimulated management to establish a relief fund for our Louisiana staff. Line staff in Philadelphia also solicited money and operated a lottery to raise more money for relief. They took this action because they felt empowered to act.

RHD's policy is that budget information is always available and open to staff for review. Salaries are not private. In addition, we mandate that the management of each unit hold a staff-wide review of its budget twice a year. Knowledge gives people power. The more the staff knows about money, the more status they have in the corporation.

Underwriting decentralization

In Chapter VI we described how RHD decentralizes its structure to equalize worth and so level the playing field among employees. Now we can look at how the corporation uses money to establish and support that decentralized structure.

In effect, we created a unitized fiscal process that gives employees the opportunity to be involved in making local fiscal decisions. It comes with clear procedures for local budget development, including line items that identify both program expenditures and overhead (that portion of the unit budget allocated to support the central system). In a for-profit this would include an allocation for profit (see Chapter IX). At this point in our development our corporate budget is subdivided into over one thousand detailed budgets.

By "profit" I am referring to earnings retained after expenditures, whether they occur in a non-profit or for-profit business. The difference between the two forms of business relates to how retained earnings are used. The non-profit cannot have individual owners and so it cannot use retained earnings to reward the "owners" (stockholders). Other than that, the non-profit can do virtually everything a for-profit does such as offer bonuses, high salaries and deferred income. At RHD we choose to use money to spread meaningful status and power. And as you know, we find it very "profitable."

Returning to the way RHD's decentralized fiscal structure works: in the contracting process, which takes place between RHD and its customers, budgets are developed that pinpoint approximately 85-87% of the total amount for unit operations. And approximately 13-15% of the total contract is used by the corporate center for administrative support and oversight. Clearly defining this administrative component within each budget makes for a transparent approach to fiscal communication. No additional centralized expenditures are hidden in unit line items. Everyone, customers and staff alike, sees how money is allocated.

As the fiscal year moves on, a Budget Manager, who is hired by the Central Office, works with a Unit Director and local fiscal staff to maintain the program. Both are responsible for assuring that budget expenditures meet established financial goals and fulfill the requirements of our customers. When this fiscal system is working as planned, however, it is the local fiscal staff and the Director, not the Budget Manager, who make daily spending decisions.

Budget Managers are the linchpins that financially connect the Central Office and the unit. Their job is to oversee, and at the same time, empower units. To do this effectively, these managers must understand that the day-to-day loyalty of RHD's 3,000 employees should be to their units, not to the Central Office. The system works wonders for our overall quality and performance.

Our eighty unit directors have an outstanding fiscal record, including keeping within budgets, and, when possible, generating retained earnings. Such earnings are not centralized; they remain with the unit to be utilized for bonuses and future unit-wide needs.

Bonuses

Unexpended unit funds are often used to give end of the year bonuses. Corporate policy indicates that such bonuses cannot be distributed to the Unit Director or to any select group alone. Instead, policy mandates that they be spread equally among all unit employees. Indeed, a few years ago, when the Central Office, itself a unit, had unexpended funds available for bonuses, I got the same $400 bonus as the 130 other employees. This is an equal worth bonus, provided to everyone as part of a work team regardless of status or different base salaries.

When corporate bonuses go to the highest paid or the most outstanding salesmen and not to a group of secretaries and shipping staff, the fact that everyone plays a part in the sales effort is denied. On the other hand, if local group efforts are valued and then rewarded, the corporation as a whole is energized.

Purchasing

Given RHD's unitized fiscal structure, you have read that almost all purchasing is done locally (see Chapter V). I have heard people criticize this approach; they usually argue that centralized purchasing is likely to be more efficient. My guess is that there are commodities used by some corporations such as steel and wood that might be significantly cheaper if bought centrally. In my view, however, there is a good likelihood that the nominal savings achieved by much centralized purchasing can also be lost due to bureaucratic inefficiency. And let's not forget the human price paid; along with centralized purchasing comes the disempowerment and frustration of those who need to make immediate on-the-job decisions. It may be more effective for a corporation to buy particular commodities centrally, while leaving local units free to purchase most supplies and to satisfy on the spot needs.

> Corporate policy indicates that such bonuses cannot be distributed to the Unit Director or to any select group alone... they will be spread equally among all unit employees.

Any corporation can follow such values-based equalizing procedures. The amount of funds involved may differ but practices such as local purchasing and equal bonuses can be maintained. They underline the reality that corporate success is a cooperative effort.

Power and status

As you know, many corporation leaders use money to enhance their own power and status. One strategy is to require that all major expenses be channeled through top management for approval. This clearly centralizes power and status. Another strategy is to keep fiscal information secret – when only the privileged few have information, they are more able to control fiscal decision-making.

If a corporation takes the common good path, the Board, the CEO and top management maintain the responsibility to develop and review overall corporate fiscal policies while Unit Directors and their associate staff have the power and the status to manage Unit budgets. If you speak to our Unit Directors, you will sense their pride in having developed and managed services that are much like small independent businesses. They attain status and power by producing quality services or products while achieving financial goals. Remember that RHD has grown from $50,000 to $162,000,000 in yearly revenue during these 37 years, and Unit Directors and their staffs have driven much of this growth.

The more that local managers are fiscally savvy and the higher their status and power, the greater is the entrepreneurial spirit of a corporation. It is this entrepreneurial spirit, tied as it is to our decentralized structure, which serves RHD so well.

Compensation and the maximum multiple

It seems obvious, but compensation is one of the most emotional areas for corporate leaders to tackle – and tackle it we must. Whatever and however compensation decisions are made, there are bound to be people who feel discounted and unappreciated. I expect to hear objections such as, "I was the one responsible for pulling that extremely important project together. How come I didn't get a special raise?"

Such questions come up repeatedly, based as they are on the belief that only one person is primarily responsible for a successful project. That person neglects to mention the support of all the people who took part in the project: the budget manager, the administrative assistant, the grant writer, the legal advisor, etc. I appreciate the role of the leader, and indeed, there is considerable status and power that comes with it. In RHD, however, we believe that success is not due to the work of one person. Instead it's the result of a remarkably effective group effort.

My own compensation is now affected by a policy that I suggested: the compensation (salary plus benefits, bonuses, options and deferred compensation) of the CEO must be capped at 14 times the compensation of the lowest paid full time RHD employee in the United States. This policy has been adopted by the Board and ratified by the staff – it will limit the growth of my compensation in the near future. At a time when corporate executives are receiving 400 to 500 times what line employees are making, I do believe that those who want to lead Common Good Corporations should set a publicly known limit to their compensation.

Fostering trust

In RHD, we assume that employees who are trained and empowered to meet financial goals can be trusted. Employee self-interest to the exclusion of corporate interest grows in direct proportion to the degree to which he or she feels not trusted, more like a cog in a wheel. That destructive self-interest reduces when everyone feels empowered to contribute and has access to the financial details.

To move us toward fulfilling the equal worth assumption, at times we determine annual salary increases by apportioning dollar amounts plus a percentage. For example, a few years ago we provided everyone in the Central Office a 2% raise plus $400. This meant that while I received a larger dollar amount than the employee who maintains our building, his raise amounted to 4% of his salary and mine was just over 2%. The decision moved toward more equalized pay. And that's powerful.

We also provide a wide range of in-house training and educational opportunities as well as a scholarship fund for those wanting to pursue formal education. Our

> ...we assume that employees who are trained and empowered to meet financial goals can be trusted.

Employee Assistance Program offers ten free counseling sessions for employees and/or their families during every year of employment. We offer organizational development services, which include facilitating services for small groups, retreats for unit staff, and coaching for administrators. Staff development curricula offer education that could lead to better positions. The corporation provides short-term disability insurance and subsidizes a credit union. Each year we sponsor a summer corporate picnic for workers and their families along with other events.

In response to the needs of the larger community, we have created RHD's Equal Dollars as a companion currency. Over 1,000 business and individual members trade goods and services with each other using equal dollars as a means of exchange. In poverty-stricken sections of Philadelphia, where US dollars are scarce, the Equal Dollars currency has more significance. And each fall we take a full day to celebrate our values. Every hour and every dollar spent on these efforts is well worth it.

Our Chief Operating Officer, Peggy Mowatt, recently led an effort to increase the benefit dollars for line staff, making it more likely that they could buy health insurance for themselves and their families. Reading what she writes about her effort, you'll get a sense of how the Common Good Corporation works toward equality and fairness.

THE BENEFITS STORY

As has been described, we treat all staff equally whenever possible. At its inception the corporation designed a benefit plan that provided exactly the same benefit formula to all eligible employees in any unit: each eligible person received 7% of his/her gross salary as additional benefit dollars.

Although this formula clearly provided more benefit dollars to the higher paid staff, it always easily covered the cost of a single person's health care for the lower paid staff. In effect, dollars were available for employees to purchase insurances such as health, life and/or disability, to put aside into an annuity for retirement, or to convert to cash as additional income. The choices were completely theirs.

Over time the benefit formulas have been changed in an effort to assure that all staff have at least enough benefit dollars to offset the cost of single health premiums. More recently, we used a 9% formula, which still meant that our higher paid staff received more benefit dollars than others.

To demonstrate this 9% formula, suppose you, as an employee working for RHD, are earning $20,000 a year. Meanwhile your Unit Director is earning $60,000. The benefit formula for your unit is 9% of gross plus $200/month. This means that RHD would contribute $4,200 per year (9% x $20,000 + 200 x 12) to you and $7,800 per year (9% x 60,000 + 200 x 12) to your Unit Director. While the benefit formula is the same, the higher paid position obviously generates more dollars. But the cost of health insurance is the same for both individuals.

If single health coverage costs $375 per month ($4,500 per year) you would incur a salary reduction to offset the difference while the Unit Director would have excess benefit dollars with which to select additional benefits. Although the plan "formula" was the same, was the result fair? Did it stand the test of our values?

Lately, as every American knows, health premium costs have increased in much greater proportion than our gross salaries. The old benefit formulas no longer provide enough money to cover the health premium costs of our lower paid staff. Individuals who need health insurance for spouses or children have had to accept significant salary reductions to cover their premium costs. Also, our program budgets, which are primarily funded by government agencies, have typically received little or no additional funding with which to simply increase everyone's benefit formula. So, we faced a dilemma. Something had to be done. We had to find ways to increase the benefit dollars available to our lower paid staff and also to those who need or want extended family health coverage.

We convened a committee to study the problem and offer solutions. This group consisted of management team members, corporate assistant directors, budget managers, unit directors, supervisors and line staff.

The group's first challenge was to reach consensus on the goals to be met. After much discussion we collectively agreed to attempt to achieve the following:

- To provide additional benefit dollars to the lower paid eligible staff;
- To provide additional benefit dollars to all employees who need to cover family members;
- To continue to permit employee "choice" in the use of their benefit dollars;
- To remain budget neutral;
- To remain competitive in the job market.

Obviously all of these goals were not compatible. Without the ability to increase the total benefit dollars available in most budgets, how would we ever increase those dollars for our lower paid staff? The debate went on for months. Ideas were proposed and abandoned as either impractical or unfair. Most ideas seemed to satisfy one goal at the direct expense of other goals. The one constant theme was fairness.

So, finally, the committee accepted the reality that to make more dollars available to lower paid staff required taking them away from our higher paid staff! It became quite clear to all committee members that we had to change the benefit formula – to reduce the percentage of gross in order to increase the health premium direct support. Remember, now, the group struggling with these issues included various RHD managers! When initially proposed, this idea was rejected out of hand. How could we take away dollars from our manager level staff without damaging their morale or, even worse, losing them? But there was no other viable solution. Once this concept was accepted as valid, the next challenge was getting managers to "de-personalize" the idea. They had to get past the negative impact they would personally experience if we made this dramatic change in benefit formula. I am very proud to say that they did, in fact, accomplish this! They recognized, but set aside, the loss they would each incur now and into the future and focused on the positive impact this would have on our lower paid staff, which they were representing in this effort.

In September of 2005, the corporate typical benefit formula changed from 9% of gross plus $200 per month toward health premium costs to 4% of gross plus a graduated support of health premium costs from $325 to $550 per month, depending on level of need. With this new formula all lower paid staff receive greater benefit dollars. Unless health costs continue to escalate at unthinkable rates, they will be much better able to provide appropriate health coverage for their families and, in many cases, have additional benefit dollars with which to consider retirement savings and/or other benefit choices.

The committee did a wonderful job! It was a difficult, time-consuming, and frequently frustrating process for all but they persevered. The result was that a new plan was approved which, although it did not fully satisfy all of the original goals, certainly accomplished the most important goal – better benefits for lower paid staff. And the entire committee concurred on the final resolution! Imagine any other corporation in the world taking benefit dollars away from higher paid staff (managers and executives) to give more to the lower paid staff (line staff workers). But we did it because it felt fairer, and I am personally very proud of everyone who participated in this effort.

As a follow-up on this story, I am happy to say that, in most program budgets, we were able to "grandfather" our existing managers' benefit dollars so that they would not lose the money they had been promised upon their earlier hire dates. All new hires, however, will enter employment at RHD with the new benefit formulas in place. This took some creative planning by budget managers to accomplish but it has certainly made the benefit transition easier for all corporate managers.

It has been my pleasure to work closely with such extraordinary leaders who strive consistently to apply the RHD values to daily decisions, whether those decisions affect a single program or the entire corporation as this one did.

CHAPTER IX

MONEY: PART TWO

In the last chapter, we examined the money tool and how it can shape internal operations. This chapter asks the question: How does a Common Good Corporation use the money produced by fiscal success?

First let's look at how individuals deal with money that is in excess of their personal needs. Many believe they can never have enough. I know an elderly woman who has $8,000,000 and she is still frightened that it will run out. Because money is associated with security and self-esteem, the need is often unquenchable. The problem is more serious when this need for more is applied to corporations.

Indeed, business people endlessly increase stockholder value because they fear being found irresponsible, and even held liable in the courts.[1] The legal history of the corporation has contributed to this problem.[2] Originally, state governments chartered certain businesses, which they called "corporations," for special civic purposes such as the construction of roads and bridges. In the name of public interest, these corporate charters protected investors from certain liabilities. For instance, a group of individuals planning to build a bridge might apply to the state for the right to incorporate. If the state government deemed the project served the common good, it would grant those individuals that right and so protected them from personal fiscal liability.

---

[1] The sale of Ben & Jerry's to Unilever.
[2] The following history is a modified version of material found in: Joel Bakan. The Corporation, Viking Canada. 2004. Thom Hartmann. Unequal Protection 2002.

And because the states feared corruption, they also regulated corporate activities.

- The corporation could only engage in activities necessary to fulfill its chartered purpose.
- A corporate charter was granted for a limited time, and charters were terminated if the corporation exceeded its authority or if it caused public harm.
- Corporate managers were responsible for criminal acts committed on the job.
- Corporations could not make any political contributions, or spend money to influence legislation.
- Corporations could not purchase or own stock in other corporations, nor could they own any property other than what was necessary to fulfill the purpose of serving the public interest.

In 1886, the Supreme Court began the long process of backing off from this regulation. The process climaxed in the 1970s when the Court declared that corporations had the same constitutional rights as individual human beings. In doing so, and in defiance of common sense and democracy, the Court undid the safeguards originally built into state corporate charters.

As a result, corporations, which were created to serve the public interest, broke free of democratic control and our country lost the legal structures that gave elected representatives the capacity to restrain corporate behavior. This meant that owners and managers were no longer accountable for a corporate social purpose, and could make as much money as possible, as quickly as possible, and use it almost entirely for personal interest. They continue to do that today.

For years I never questioned this approach to corporate fiscal management. The practice seemed as natural as breathing air. Now I understand that the sole focus on making money is dangerous.

I hope that one day the Supreme Court will revisit the idea that corporations have the same rights as individuals. This law does not, and cannot, serve the common good. The reality is that a corporation is not a person; as an institution, it doesn't have the human capacity to carefully and responsibly use the money tool. It doesn't have the capacity to balance the needs of the corporation with a concern for workers, consumers, and its community. The Supreme Court needs to redefine corporate rights within the framework of the Constitution so that corporations will once again be responsible for balancing business activity with the common good.

Until that happens, corporate stakeholders, including owners, workers, and consumers, need to be wary of anyone who justifies a corporation's endless pursuit of money by arguing for corporate need. That's like saying the hammer I'm swinging is demanding that I break a few windows. It also implies that I'm not in control of the hammer, and, therefore, not responsible.

Since the Supreme Court and our state governments are not doing this work, this is a time for stakeholders to take clear responsibility for how their corporations accumulate and use their money. To do this, they need a values-based process for managing the money that large corporations are now accruing. It's of vital interest to all of us.

> ...this is a time for stakeholders to take clear responsibility for how their corporations accumulate and use their money.

THE CORPORATE MONEY TOOL BOX

Money, like the hammer, comes in various forms and we need different kinds of hammers to do different jobs. For instance, it would be dangerous to choose a sledgehammer with an eight-pound head to put a very small nail in the wall. Similarly, corporate leaders need to match the kind of money used with the job to be done. Householders do that all the time when they identify food money, vacation money, or rent money.

Now let's identify the different kinds of money that are in the corporate toolbox, and how each of them is used. For instance, corporations have *operations money*, funds appropriated to run the business. And if a corporation is successful, it will also have *discretionary money*, those funds that remain after all operating expenses plus taxes, principal and interest on debt are paid. Some portion of corporate discretionary money expenditures are identified as *before tax*, while other discretionary money expenditures *shelter tax*. To simplify, I suggest we always measure the amount of the discretionary money used for specific purposes as a percentage of total discretionary money available in the corporate tax year *before taxes or capitalization*.

This analysis doesn't deal with employee salaries and benefits since they are usually considered part of a corporation's operating expenses. For this reason, this discussion does not include the extraordinarily high salaries that certain managers receive, therefore lowering the amount of corporate discretionary money available for others. To explore this issue, see Money: Part I, where I suggest the use of a "maximum multiple."

Now we will take a closer look at discretionary money. I suggest that it falls into three categories, each describing a different kind of expenditure.

DISCRETIONARY MONEY

Corporate money, our first category, is used for payments to owners and for bonuses, options or "perks" to key managers. It is also used for expenditures that add to the value of the corporation such as the upgrading of buildings or the purchasing of machinery and computers. Corporate money keeps businesses vital, current and competitive. Determining how much discretionary money goes in this category is a question of values. This point is extremely important because Corporate Money expenditures are usually appropriated first and often consume most of an organization's discretionary money. As a result little is left for categories that are the cornerstones of the Common Good Corporation.

Worker money is used for activities that transfer cash or benefits into the lives of employees. This is money that is appropriated beyond government requirements and contract agreements with unions. It is money that corporate leaders *choose* to spend on expenditures and activities. It can change year by year.

Community money is used to enrich communities that are external to the corporation itself. Community money could include the creation of sports fields, the support of arts institutions, and a variety of non-profit activities. This money might also include pollution control or environmentally sound uses of energy. These are all efforts that move beyond those prescribed by law.

The public usually isn't aware of the existence of corporate discretionary money, let alone how it is distributed across these three categories. Public knowledge, is essential to the Common Good Corporation, since such money

Determining how much discretionary money goes in this category is a question of values.

allows stakeholders to make conscious choices. The categories make clear what is usually opaque.

In the analysis below I offer eleven sub-categories to differentiate how corporate discretionary money is, or can be, used. To further illustrate these sub-categories, I will then talk about RHD's use of discretionary money between July 2004 and June 2005. Finally, we will once again return to the three broad categories and further explore a common good approach to corporate discretionary money.

CORPORATE DISCRETIONARY MONEY: SUB-CATEGORIES
Corporate Money

- **Corporate money-1** Funds retained by the corporation in the form of cash or cash equivalents to increase net value.

- **Corporate money-2** Funds distributed to owners as profits and dividends, and funds distributed to top managers as bonuses, options or "perks" during the year.

- **Corporate money-3** Funds used for infrastructure improvements and/or purchases such as machinery, buildings, computer systems and telephone systems.

- **Corporate money-4** Funds retained by the corporation for acquisition of businesses for expansion or diversification.

- **Corporate money-5** Funds used for research, development and marketing costs for all new products or services.

Worker Money

- **Worker money-1** Funds used to provide benefits (beyond those mandated by government or union contracts, including "cafeteria plans"). The category also includes insurance, education, employee health services, conference attendance, picnics or celebrations, etc. This is a major use of discretionary funds within Common Good Corporations.

- **Worker money-2** Funds used to provide additional amenities and facilities such as day care, exercise rooms, health care on site, etc.

- **Worker money-3** Funds used to provide bonuses including those based on surpluses or profits.

Community Money

- **Community money-1** Funds used for remediation of environmental problems beyond legal requirements.

- **Community money-2** Funds used to provide the community with facilities such as sports fields, transportation, theaters, etc.

- **Community money-3** Funds used to make donations to improve the well being of people. This is often accomplished via contributions to non-profit corporations, governmental entities, or individuals.

This list of the uses of discretionary money is not intended to be exhaustive, and each corporation is likely to define these categories somewhat differently. The categories do, however, provide us with a framework to understand how a particular corporation distributes discretionary money within the eleven categories. Then we can compare how different corporations balance their distribution of discretionary money across the larger three categories.

Clearly, corporations produce varying amounts of discretionary funds dependent on the profit margins involved in their various products. Even so, the percent balance between the three larger categories can be compared from corporation to corporation. Not only is this informative, it also allows us to consider a common good approach to managing discretionary money.

As the CEO of a large corporation, I want to emphasize my appreciation of the fact that owners and managers need "sufficient" funds within the Corporate Money category. Strong and effective arguments can be made for allocations in each of the five Corporate Money categories. I have done the same over the years and would do so today. So, let's not take the time to debate whether a corporation should use money to acquire other corporations (Corporate Money-4,) or if it should invest in Research, Development and Sales

(Corporate Money-5). Let's also agree that bonuses for top management (Corporate Money-2) are recognized as a common monetary tool to motivate individuals; and in certain industries, such allocations are a part of contract negotiations. These debates are important in themselves but please recall that the final question is: *How much is enough?*

It's also important to note that many non-profit corporations regularly produce discretionary funds, and non-profit hospitals and universities, as well as organizations like RHD, don't pay federal or local taxes on them.

Since these non-profits do not have owners, they do not use Corporate Money-2 funds for distribution to shareholders. However, Corporate Money-2 funds are often used for bonuses for top management or key sales people. (Given our values-based culture, RHD is an exception.) Many of us, as well as the IRS, are now questioning the percentage of discretionary funds used by non-profits such as Harvard University and The New York Stock Exchange with Corporate Money-1 and Corporate Money-2 activities to increase the corporate net worth or for the salaries and bonuses provided to management. All the other categories apply to for-profit and non-profit businesses equally.

My basic point is that if stakeholders want to establish a Common Good Corporation, whether for-profit or non-profit, they need to debate such decisions. As a stakeholder in a corporation, for instance, you might want to consider the balance of distribution between the categories of discretionary funds. You may also wonder whether there are, or can be, opportunities for stakeholders to openly review, debate, and re-balance such decisions. And is it possible for stakeholders who don't have an ownership and/or management interest in the corporation to have this opportunity? This year? Next year?

RHD AND DISCRETIONARY MONEY

Now let's turn to RHD. Using the categories proposed it's possible to examine how one Common Good Corporation balances its allocations among Corporate, Worker, and Community Money. During the fiscal year between July 2004 and June 2005, RHD identified a total of $12,311,341 in discretionary corporate funds. During that same fiscal year, RHD enjoyed gross revenues of

$112,509,000. After operating expenses, RHD used its discretionary money in the following ways.

- Corporate Money: 32%
- Worker Money: 63%
- Community Money: 05 %

....

- Worker and Community
  Money combined: 68%

The balance between the three categories combined clearly tilts toward the combination of the last two categories.

RHD DISCRETIONARY MONEY: DISTRIBUTION ACROSS SUB-CATEGORIES

Corporate Money

- **Corporate money-1** Funds retained   941,744
- **Corporate money-2** Owner profits and management bonuses   0
- **Corporate money-3** Infrastructure improvements, purchases   2,377,000
- **Corporate money-4** Acquisition of businesses   0
- **Corporate money-5** Research, development, marketing   665,384

Worker Money

- **Worker money-1** Benefits beyond those mandated   7,068,809
- **Worker money-2** Additional workplace amenities   640,037
- **Worker money-3** Bonuses based on profits   0

(Workers may get a bonus from their units)

Community Money

- **Community money-1** Alleviation of environmental problems   7,980
- **Community money-2** Community facilities   106,176
- **Community money-3** Donations for well-being of people   504,213

Total $12,311,341

It's clear that RHD management has chosen to put most of RHD's discretionary funds into worker money ($7,708,844 or 63%) in the form of additional benefits. While this does help the corporation attract staff, our primary intent as a Common Good Corporation is to enhance Worker Money whenever funds can be made available.

Secondly, if you look at the details above, it becomes clear that a number of Corporate Money expense lines have not been funded, even though a total of $3,984,128 (32%) is allocated for this use. This is possible because RHD makes it a practice to restrict its financial rewards for top management and to limit the funds retained to increase corporate wealth.

Most corporations cannot or would not choose to allocate such a small percentage of discretionary funds into the corporate money category given the pressure from owners who often wish that they or their corporation would be rich beyond all need. However, it's a pressure that needs to be resisted.

I believe all stakeholders, including managers, line workers, consumers, and community members affected by corporations, need a voice in the distribution of corporate wealth. The absence of such a debate leaves management with a power that has often been handled without any sensitivity to the civic responsibilities that corporate charters should address.

Lastly, the very figures printed above demonstrate that the disclosure of corporate discretionary funds, along with how they are allocated, is essential to stimulate debate in a Common Good Corporation. While both owners and managers covet for-profit and non-profit corporate discretionary funds, this chapter argues that other less well-informed groups also have a claim to be in on the debate.

I suggest that those of us who wish to further the democratic nature of our society have an obligation to educate these poorly informed groups and to include them in the debate about how corporate wealth is used. In this way, managers and owners have the opportunity to nourish our democratic nation. It's a fulfilling, joyful experience.

> ...all stakeholders, including managers, line workers, consumers, and community members affected by corporations, need a voice in the distribution of corporate wealth.

CAPITAL TO PEOPLE

Capital to People (CP) is the name of a for-profit investment fund that is controlled by RHD and used for community economic development activities— in particular to create sustainable, living wage jobs for low-income people. We do this with the recognition that the poor, and in particular poor minorities, lack the robust economic platform from which to launch small businesses. At best such a platform would include an infrastructure with adequate sources of capital, cash flow financing, accessible and proven expertise, adequate supply chains, and lastly, customers with the money to buy. The CP system is an attempt to provide member small businesses with components of that economic platform.

Can you think of a better way for a mature corporation to use *discretionary* money than to invest in a business that aims at improving conditions in its community? I can't. The effort is part of our community contribution. It's not a big stretch to say that other corporations could also set aside some percentage of their discretionary money to work on such projects in the communities that surround them. Sometimes these efforts contribute to the corporation's positive bottom line. Whether or not that happens, they are very likely to improve the positive reputation of their business – beyond anything that an advertising campaign can buy. And it feels great to support people like Tim, the entrepreneur who started Service Works. Now he tells the story!

SERVICE WORKS

Service Works is a custodial service that currently has a workforce of over 80 highly trained, skilled and motivated employees who deliver superior janitorial services. By design, employees actively participate in almost all levels of the business. For instance, new hires are interviewed by a committee of workers, and then join a self-directed work team that chooses its own coach. This self-directed team is then trained to perform managerial tasks such as scheduling, customer relations, equipment management and general training of new staff. Service Works has an employee culture that is more customer-aware and less authoritarian, all of which goes a long way toward raising the status of service workers in the eyes of each service employee and the public at large.

Capital to People has invested considerable time and consulting services in Service Works. It also invested $200,000 and used an additional $100,000 as security for a credit line.

When I think of what it took to be a small entrepreneur developing Service Works, three qualities come to mind: persistence, courage and insanity. Persistence is primary. It has taken me close to ten years to learn the skills needed to be a successful entrepreneur. Courage comes next. Believe me, I've had my fair share of failure. And each time it has happened, I had to have the courage to pick myself up and try again.

Lastly I have to say that anyone who is an entrepreneur, including me, has to be a little crazy. Riding the entrepreneurial rollercoaster with its extreme ups and downs, and knowing that over 90% of small businesses fail, takes an optimism bordering on insanity.

Our first contract was with a supermarket chain. The memory warms my heart. I hired guys from Always Have A Dream (AHAD), which is an RHD drug and alcohol recovery program. We bought a small van and worked 6 days a week going from one supermarket to another refinishing floors. I am proud to say that our call-out rate was less than 1% and our turnover rate was less than 30%.

I also began to market our janitorial service to other suburban companies, and developed a transportation system to bring employees from the city to do those jobs. Service Works hired low-income people including mothers on welfare, addicts in recovery and ex-convicts. One of the most important things I learned in the early years was how to choose people who were likely to be successful employees.

Being hired, however, is just the first step for whoever works for us. Service Works employees get medical benefits, access to an employee assistance program, and a raise after their first 90 days. And that's not all. We attend to the barriers to employment. If an employee can't come to work, they're encouraged to tell me and I might pay them for personal leave. If a worker needs childcare or family-care to hold on to a job, we help make that happen. If transportation is a problem, we find a way to work that out. We go even further with those whose families are torn apart; for example, if an employee is living separately from his wife, or his wife living separately from one or all of her children, we try to help make their families whole.

Given this approach to staff, I'm proud to say that over 70% of those we hired over the last ten years are still working – whether at Service Works or elsewhere. My own staff average is 6 years of employment. And we don't have an absentee problem. Yesterday we had 2 call-outs with 84 employees at work. In fact, one of our challenges is to tell people that, because of labor laws, they need to leave work after the day is over! For all these reasons, Service Works has a more stable and a more skilled workforce than the ones I managed years ago for several large academic institutions.

Over the years I've spent as an entrepreneur, I have had a number of mind-altering insights. For instance, I learned that an ex-con who is 40 years old or older, perhaps someone who has committed a felony when he was a teenager or young adult, is likely to be a good employee. If I treat him well, he is likely to treat the company and our consumers well. At this point, about 90% of my management team is mature ex-offenders. They make good leaders.

I also learned that I wasn't clear about the needs of my customers. I thought that they would contract with us because we were socially responsible, but most companies didn't care about that. After 9/11 when corporations began instituting draconian security procedures – if one of my employees had committed a felony in the past 20 years (it used to be 5 years), he couldn't be hired. Of course, this policy flew in the face of what I had learned about the reliability of older ex-cons, but that didn't matter.

And I learned that many corporate managers did not want to buy services from someone with a black face. Was it because they were prejudiced? Was it a conscious choice? Or was it simply that people are more likely to trust those who look like them? I think all these possibilities have some truth to them. It meant that I had to partner with white-faced people to angle us into the market.

Meanwhile, the Bush administration is currently making a big effort to do business with minority firms – of course that's the law, but this administration is enforcing it. And the local Philadelphia government is doing the same. I recently received city certification as a minority business. That will help. Now we are applying for federal certification. The binder for this application is at least 8 inches thick – and extremely complicated. However, the certification will go a long way toward making us successful.

And I'm proud to say that I recently received an award for the best minority business of 2005 for Pennsylvania. It came from the Minority Business Development Association, which is funded by the US Department of Commerce. Along with the award came a scholarship for a week of intensive executive education at the Tuck School of Business at Dartmouth College. They focused on me and on my company, and for the next three years they will chart my progress.

I also continue to have Capital to People behind me. They help in many ways – by offering the financial analyses any business needs, through consultation on business strategies, and by providing cash flow when necessary and at times on an emergency basis to meet payroll when receivables are late in coming.

134

CHAPTER X

THE FOR-PROFIT CROSSOVER

Both the non-profit corporation and the for-profit corporation are remarkably powerful economic tools. While the former is tax-free and able to receive grants, the latter is designed to attract the capital needed for business activities. When both are used they can stimulate an infinite range of economic activities, and generate sufficient discretionary revenue to address business as well as social issues. Therefore I suggest that every non-profit common good corporation create one or more for-profit corporations – and use them to attract the capital needed to invest in businesses that can address a social agenda.

Given the level of funding for non-profits, their social agendas are limited to providing care for people who have fallen off the cliff; some are chronically unemployed, others are mentally ill, developmentally disabled, or in recovery from an addiction to drugs or alcohol. Many have had years of inadequate health care and sub-standard educational opportunities.

I have no doubt that, overall, non-profits do their best to help these people climb back up that cliff, but given their broken minds and bodies, and the minimal resources available, only a limited number can make it. Counseling cannot adequately speak to an economic or an educational problem. Retraining cannot adequately address the pay scales that make supporting a family impossible. And health care for a medical problem that has never been treated well can rarely speak to a spirit that has given up. For these reasons I believe that we need to

> I suggest that every non-profit common good corporation create one or more for-profit corporations– and use them to attract the capital needed to invest in businesses that address a social agenda.

reach people before they have fallen off the cliff, and it is the for-profit corporation that is more likely to have the financial resources to do this job.

Since the 1980s, I have been keenly interested in an ingenious economic breakthrough called The Mondragon Cooperative System, which is based in the Basque region of Spain.[1] It is the best example I know of common good investments by a system of for-profit businesses. Father Don Jose Arizmendiarrieta and five young engineers started Mondragon in 1956. By 2005 it had over 264 separate corporations and 70,000 workers and its sales exceeded $18 billion euros per year.

> The Mondragon Cooperative System...is the best example I know of common good investments by a system of for-profit businesses.

While developing businesses, the Mondragon cooperative system has also addressed the social needs of its community by developing a research institute, over 40 schools, a college, a health maintenance system, and a health insurance system. Mondragon also has a cooperative central banking system, which offers a prime example of the *patient capital* I refer to later in this chapter. The bank not only lends money at modest rates for capitalization and cash flow, but also provides refinancing for a business that needs to be restructured. During this restructuring, payments on past loans might be suspended and consultation provided to help open new markets.

Mondragon is particularly interested in businesses that are begun by groups. The assumption is that a group pulling together, rather than an individual entrepreneur leading the effort, is more likely to produce success – a remarkable shift from the faith Americans place in an individual entrepreneur. It is also required that the new business leaders and the central bank consultants continue to work together until the enterprise is profitable.

In this model forty percent of profits are used to enrich the company, ten percent is set aside for community needs, and the remaining fifty percent goes into worker accounts. The latter is kept in the central bank and used to help other Mondragon businesses. Last but not least, all workers share a stake in the ownership. Given Mondragon's success, it's clear that broad stakeholder participation is having a remarkable effect.

For many years I have had the dream of developing a business system similar to Mondragon because Father Arizmendiarrieta's business model made a profit and

---

[1] Morrison, Roy (1991) *We Build The Road As We Travel.* Philadelphia, PA .: New Society Publishers. www.mondragon.mcc.es/ing/estructura/estructura.html

also served the common good. That is exactly what I want to do in our country. Indeed, Mondragon was in the forefront of my mind when RHD took its first steps into the for-profit world through the creation of Murex Corporation.

The need for Murex Corporation emerged from RHD's participation in the development of The Please Touch Museum for children in Philadelphia. The museum's rapid growth led us to seek additional space within the building that housed it. However, the national corporation that owned the building wanted a multi-year lease, thus placing RHD at risk if the museum could not sustain itself. In order to protect RHD and the museum, the managing group decided to set up a "shell" corporation.

In effect, we established a for-profit corporation to rent the space, knowing that if the museum went south, we could limit Murex's funding and allow it to go bankrupt. The Murex name was suggested by the museum's founder, who reasoned that since this would be a shell corporation it might as well be named after a shell – the murex shell, which in ancient times was used to produce the purple dye to color the robes of royalty.

With Murex Corporation in place, RHD's leadership began to enter into numerous business and tax credit partnerships, using the structure to raise millions to finance housing for the elderly, the homeless, and for the disabled. RHD was on a path that allowed the non-profit to have a significant stake in for-profit corporations in order to engage in constructive community work. Much like Mondragon, Murex Corporation invests money in new businesses only if they are likely to achieve social as well as financial goals. And although we have focused on minority and female ownership, profit sharing and employee ownership have been included in many deals.

Sometimes Murex Corporation will offer a business *impatient capital*, namely a short-term loan with interest. It requires a quick return of principal and interest. Alternatively, Murex will also invest *patient capital* in a business. This capital allows for the time and flexibility that most start-up businesses need. When offering patient capital Murex is likely to limit its financial returns on invested funds to 3%, and set a long time period for exit, or no planned exit, from the investment. This time and return flexibility is unique and allows Murex to

> Much like Mondragon, Murex Corporation invests money in new businesses only if they are likely to achieve social as well as financial goals.

consider businesses with strong social agendas that would be rejected by both the banking system and venture funds. Mondragon also uses capital in a very patient way when it suspends payments on old loans, and simultaneously puts new capital into businesses because they require restructuring.

When offering patient capital, Murex is likely to limit its financial returns on invested funds to 3% and set a long time period for exit, or no planned exit, from the investment.

In our country business ventures run a high rate of failure because they can only access impatient capital. Might the American government and for-profit investors consider setting aside a small portion of their funds for use as patient capital? I certainly think they should.

Mondragon and RHD are similar in regard to the commitment to their corporations, their workers and communities. Mondragon uses a portion of its profits to capitalize the corporation, as does RHD through its Corporate Money Fund category. Both Mondragon and RHD set the largest percentage aside to enrich workers, and so does RHD through its Worker Money Fund. Lastly, Mondragon requires that 10% of a company's profits be allocated to the community, and so does RHD through its Community Money Fund (see chapter IX). Mondragon has experienced only a 3% failure rate for start-up companies over the last thirty years they have been in existence, while in our country we tolerate a 90% failure rate for new companies in their first ten years. Perhaps RHD's and Mondragon's successes have something in common.

In one example of the use of patient capital, over a decade ago Murex had the opportunity to invest in a start-up with a female entrepreneur who established a computer sales and repair business called Computer Systems and Solutions. In the deal between the entrepreneur and Murex the entrepreneur owned 70% of the partnership. Please note that Murex made a considered decision to use patient capital and to negotiate for a minority share of the business. The intent was to empower the entrepreneur.

In this business model profits were not tied to the percentage of ownership. Instead, Murex and the entrepreneur agreed that when profits exceeded a pre-set amount within a year, 8% would be set aside for non-profit social goals. Recently the partners were able to profitably sell a portion of the business. The sale led to contributions to the non-profit of over $15,000 in 2005. This is how patient capital can serve business and the community.

IMPATIENT AND PATIENT CAPITAL

Impatient capital, which drives our economy and often produces serious destabilizing results, differs from patient capital by pressuring owners and leaders to:

- Maximize returns in the shortest possible time in order to increase the return to investors and top managers through quick sales, mergers and outsourcing while cutting labor and supply chain costs.
- Externalize any and all social problems that a business activity might produce. For many business people the word "externalize" translates into: "It's not our problem."

Patient capital encourages owners and leaders to:

- Focus on long-term sustainability of a corporation rather than quick sale, merger, or outsourcing.
- Consider contracts that provide sufficient support to businesses in a corporation's supply chain to avoid business failures in that chain.
- Allocate a percentage of profits to employees.
- Allocate a percentage of profits for community needs and the amelioration of negative environmental and social impact due to corporate activity.

Clearly, the sources of patient capital determine the degree of risk that can be taken, the required return on funds, and the length of time that the capital can be left in the business. RHD and the Murex systems receives patient capital funds; for instance, we have received grants from federal, state, and local governments, private foundations, public corporations, and individuals that permit us to invest or loan without any exit strategy or return requirements. This money comes with a range of stipulations, often requiring the commitment to invest in particular communities. Nevertheless, such funding obviously permits the widest latitude for use, which makes it very valuable as a public policy initiative.

Patient capital funds can also be raised when investors understand that the funds will be at risk, and the return will be capped at a particularly low IRR (internal rate of return). For instance, private individuals, as well as RHD, have invested funds through Murex that have been capped at 3%. Any number of interest targets can be defined. However, given the need to include social goals, patient capital cannot seek the highest rate of return.

Currently, Murex Corporation manages a $1 million patient capital fund. While this fund is 15 years old and has ownership positions in a few businesses, I still consider it to be in a very early stage of development. Meanwhile, Murex Investment Corporation has recently established a $17 million Small Business Administration sponsored equity venture fund. It is also developing additional investment pools that require returns, and therefore are classified as impatient funds.

The Double Bottom Line

The practices I have written about are not RHD's alone. They are part of a larger socially responsible business effort to seek the "double bottom line" to balance profit making with a social agenda. As a corporate member of the Social Venture Network and Investor's Circle RHD joins with other entrepreneurs across the nation who are making the link between profit and the common good. Ben & Jerry's Ice Cream, Stonyfield Yogurt, The Body Shop, The White Dog Café and UnTours in Philadelphia as well as many others balance profit-making with such important efforts as organic farming, local purchasing, worker ownership, and ecological awareness. In this movement common good business people talk to others who think similarly. The support we get from each other is invaluable.

It is my hope that every for-profit common good corporation will establish joint ventures with at least one non-profit corporation. I also suggest that every for-profit establish a separately incorporated patient capital fund, which can be capitalized with tax-deductible donations of stock or cash to enable a social agenda. And like Murex Investments, any for-profit common good corporation can set the rules for ownership and the distribution of profits on business endeavors so that they meet particular interests.

To end this chapter I offer a description of a current Murex business venture that includes all the components of a common good for-profit corporation with one new addition: namely, that a separate foundation has been established to manage and donate a significant part of the profits.

> The practices I have written about are not RHD's alone. They are part of a larger socially responsible business effort to see the "double bottom line" to balance profit-making with a social agenda.

140

Recently Murex launched SQA Pharmacy Services, Inc. (SQA) in an effort to increase the quality of care for RHD's consumers who suffer from severe disabilities. Half of the stock is owned by a foundation that will use a considerable portion of SQA's profits to improve the health of those who lack health insurance. For me, launching SQA is an opportunity to model a socially responsible for-profit company that places financial gain and social return on an equal footing. Stan, an assistant to me, tells the story.

❦

SQA PHARMACY SERVICES, INC.
PROVIDING SERVICE, QUALITY AND ACCURACY

The motivation to develop SQA arose when RHD's Access Team, in-house professional consultants, took a close look at medication administration and pharmaceutical services across several units of the corporation, and found certain difficulties in this vital aspect of consumer care. It appeared that local drug stores were not offering the necessary services. A team of staff and consultants then decided to test a relationship between RHD and a closed-door pharmacy, which provided drugs and services solely to health and residential-care facilities. The test introduced individual pill packaging and labeling. The outcome of this two-year effort was a significant decrease in medication errors.

The project piqued Bob's interest. Perhaps, he thought, RHD could run its own closed-door pharmacy. And the number of RHD consumers appeared to be sizable enough so that a pharmacy that was answerable to units would have an immediate effect on quality of care across the corporation. Bob also recognized that a for-profit closed-door pharmacy primarily owned by RHD's Murex Corporation and the aforementioned foundation would allow for a significant share of the profits to be used for social purposes.

In the subsequent due diligence conducted by the Murex staff, it became apparent that the spread between operating expenses and the pricing structure

> Launching SQA is an opportunity to model a socially responsible for-profit company that places financial gain and social return on an equal footing.

was such that this pharmacy could make a 21% profit, thus justifying the investment of capital needed. RHD's bank expressed an interest in providing the cash flow funding.

Financial modeling established a foundation and determined that it would initially own 50% of SQA and 75% within five years. According to our plan, all of the dividends and distributions received by this foundation would be used to provide grants to cover the costs of improved health care for those who had no third party coverage. Murex itself will initially own 16% of SQA and 25% within five years. This distribution of stock contrasts sharply with other closed pharmacies in which virtually all stock is owned privately. In SQA a true double bottom line, financial and social, is being created.

From a business standpoint, SQA promised to be a sound investment particularly because of its link to a non-profit. The fact is that as long as SQA serves RHD's consumers well, it has an assured market. And the numbers are impressive for a start-up company: in Philadelphia and its surrounding counties RHD serves over seven hundred consumers who, taken together, need over 4,000 prescriptions filled each month. These consumers suffer from severe disabilities that prevent them from buying and managing their own medication.

In the summer of 2006 the SQA Pharmacy and the SQA Foundation became legal entities. And our initial financing, which includes a $250,000 equity investment and $650,000 for working capital, was put in place. We also hired a Pharmacy Director and an operating pharmacist along with other personnel.

SQA began operations in September of 2006. Following the business plan its services were, and still are, tailor-made to fit the needs of each unit and its consumers. The pharmacy offers periodic training for caregivers on how to dispense various medications as well as an emergency service for filling and delivering prescriptions in crisis situations. In addition, the pharmacy staff is actively designing and providing operating systems for residential staff so as to improve efficiency and produce clear records.

SQA has an Advisory Board composed of people who have a stake in customer service including several unit directors, nurses, and others who provide medications to our consumers. We are also developing relationships with identified customer service personnel at each unit, thus maintaining direct contact with RHD's staff and their consumers. Excellent quality care is fundamental to any sustainable business.

We expect to break even by the end of the first year of business. And shortly after we distribute dividends and create the social/financial impact that was planned.

As the CEO of a non-profit I see SQA as a Robin Hood solution to the problems that the poor and ill have in accessing necessary health care. The pharmacy is also an important first step in modeling a for-profit owned by a non-profit that is distributing significant profits to an array of social agencies to benefit the public. The combination of these two forms of business can bring needed funding to organizations that are chronically in distress given their dependency on grants and tax-supported contracts. Perhaps SQA will stimulate entrepreneurs to use their American business savvy to think of still other models that both make money and attend to the common good.

144

CONCLUSION

I n 1943 when Thomas Watson, Chairman of IBM was asked about the potential market for computers he said, "I think there is a world market for maybe five computers."

In 1981 when Bill Gates was asked how much memory might be needed in a computer he observed, "640K ought to be enough for anybody."

It is also said that corporations do not have any purpose other than to make a profit. Indeed, most business people believe that large corporations cannot contribute to positive social change and be economically successful. This book is my effort to show this belief to be as faulty as the predictions of Bill Gates and Thomas Watson.

Many people somehow believe they can predict the future despite evidence to the contrary. I often pay attention to such predictions – particularly negative ones – when I describe a new project idea or a new approach to corporate life. That is, when the person I happen to be talking to says that it cannot possibly work. Because I have grown to expect this reaction to the new, I settle in to listen closely and at best learn something important. But I am careful not to absorb the negative predictions about a future possibility.

The same is true for many of us who accept the RHD culture. We do not let negative predictions about actions deriving from common good values or negativism towards out-of-the-box ideas interfere with celebrating the possible. This is one of the major reasons that RHD's experiment has worked.

I invite you to celebrate the possible with us. Let's create many different kinds of common good corporations. How?

- First and foremost, let us believe that we can do it together.
- Let us create a brand called the "common good corporation" and use the brand name repeatedly to refer to our work together; in this way building many corporations that achieve the economic success that includes positive social change.
- Let us introduce, define, and implement common good corporate values and practices in the businesses we are currently developing or helping others to develop.
- Let us ask questions about policies and behaviors that trouble us wherever we work, and promote the values we would like in our own work environments – whatever they are and wherever we work.

Please understand that when you begin to talk about the often-unstated values that drive your corporation's management of people, power and money, many of your colleagues will look at you as though your comments make no sense. Many people have a hard time believing that values can be made operational and used to create change. It might seem to them that you are coming from another world because these conversations rarely take place in corporate settings.

However, if you share excerpts from this book, our experiment and its success can help you to demonstrate that such talk not only makes sense, it can go a long way towards creating economic success.

There are other processes that you can consider using. You can ask others to join you in a discussion that is now occurring, or start a new one on our web site: **www.commongoodcorporation.org.**

As you know the RHD experiment includes a number of unique components. Each one is likely to be re-shaped to fit the needs of another corporation. We can, however, use the RHD example to clarify the minimum requirements for each component. Any change in how people, power and money are managed is a success – as long as the direction is, in your and your group's judgment, a positive step.

You can also challenge your fellow workers to join a local discussion group. Working together members can write down the values operating in their organization and suggest alternatives.

Challenge your fellow employees to consider whether they want to continue working under current conditions or if they want to promote change. And invite them to be a part of that change.

And please, it is important to remember, and remind others, that this is not an effort to work against managers and owners, but rather to engage them in a process that includes all stakeholders. If the corporation is to have a common good environment, continued growth, and ongoing financial success, managers and owners, as well as workers, must be a part of the process. This is a win/win effort.

Along the way please keep contact with us via our web site about the work you and others are doing. And use the web site to search for clarity, support, and the insights of others. If you are already on this journey, we would like to hear from you. Join in this effort, along with others, to share your ideas and offer your support. Let's see what we can do!

Bob Fishman

BIBLIOGRAPHY

Argyris, Chris. <u>Interpersonal Competence and Organizational Effectiveness.</u> USA: The Dorsey Press, Inc., 1962.

Argyris, Chris, and Schon, Donald, A., <u>Theory in Practice: Increasing Professional Effectiveness.</u> San Francisco: Jossey-Bass Publishers, 1976.

Bakan, Joel. <u>The Corporation: The Pathological Pursuit of Profit and Power.</u> Canada: Viking, 2004.

Bennis, Warren, G. <u>Changing Organizations: Essays on The Development and Evolution of Human Organization.</u> USA: McGraw-Hill, Inc., 1966.

Block, Peter. <u>Stewardship: Choosing Service Over Self-Interest.</u> Berrett-Koehler Publishers, Inc., 1993.

Cohen, Ben, and Warwick, Mal. <u>Values-Driven Business: How to Change The World, Make Money, and Have Fun.</u> USA: Berrett-Koehler, 2006.

Erasmus, Charles, J. <u>In Search Of The Common Good.</u> New York: The Free Press, 1977.

<u>Figuring Out The Fed: Answers To The Most Frequently Asked Questions About The Federal Reserve System.</u> Compiled by Thoren, Margaret. USA: Truth In Money, Inc., Revised Second Edition, 1993.

Gates, Jeff. <u>Democracy At Risk</u>: Rescuing Main Street From Wall Street. USA: Perseus Publishing, 2000.

Gates, Jeff. <u>The Ownership Solution: Toward a Shared Capitalism for the 21st Century.</u> Reading, Maine: 1998.

Gates, Jeff. <u>Zapp! The Lightning of Empowerment.</u> New York: Ballantine Books, 1988.

Gesell, Silvio. <u>The Natural Economic Order.</u> Copyright 1909. Translated by Philip Pye M.A.: London: Peter Owen Ltd., 1958.

Gleick, James. <u>Chaos: Making A New Science.</u> New York: Penguin Books, 1987.

Greider, William. <u>Secrets of the Temple: How The Federal Reserve Runs The Country.</u> New York: Touchstone: 1987.

Hartmann, Thom. <u>Unequal Protection: The Rise of Corporate Dominance and The Theft of Human Rights.</u> USA: Rodale Inc., 2002.

Hawken, Paul. <u>The Next Economy.</u> New York; Holt, Rinehart and Winston, 1983.

MacLeod, Greg. <u>From Mondragon To America: Experiments in Community Economic Development.</u> Nova Scotia: University College of Cape Breton Press, 1997.

McGregor, Douglas. <u>The Human Side of Enterprise: Annotated Edition.</u> USA: The McGraw-Hill Companies, 2006.

Morrison, Roy. <u>We Build The Road As We Travel.</u> Philadelphia: New Society Publishers. 1991.

Swann, Robert and Witt, Susan. <u>Local Currencies: Catalysts for Sustainable Regional Economies.</u> USA: E.F. Schumacher Society, 1995.

Weisbord, Marvin, R. <u>Productive Workplaces: Organizing and Managing for Dignity, Meaning, and Community.</u> San Francisco: Jossey-Bass Publishers, 1987.

RESOURCES
FOR
HUMAN DEVELOPMENT, INC.

Bill of Rights and Responsibilities
For Employees and Consumers

Resources for Human Development, Inc.

4700 Wissahickon Avenue

Philadelphia, PA 19144-4248

Tel: 215.951.0300

INTRODUCTION

The values of RHD make us a unique organization. They give us rights as well as responsibilities. In order to really live the values, we need to incorporate them into everything we do. It is not always easy, but the RHD *Bill of Rights and Responsibilities for Employees and Consumers* is there to help guide us in living these values. The values are ours only if we step up to the challenge and make them work, together.

The RHD *Bill of Rights and Responsibilities* is actually a collection of writings developed over the past two decades that, together, serve as the framework for the culture we strive to create and maintain within RHD. We strongly encourage each employee to carefully read and think about the articles that comprise the document, and to participate actively in making the RHD environment in which he or she works reflect the Bill's spirit and intent.

September 2006

RHD ORGANIZATIONAL VALUES
(CONDENSED VERSION)

RHD is a values-driven organization. We no not merely encourage all members of the corporation to support and promote the organizational values; we **require** that they do so. Although there are a number of values that are important to the organization, certain values serve as its cornerstone:

Respect for the Dignity and Worth of Each Individual - Employees and consumers have the right to live and/or work in an environment that affirms their fundamental dignity as human beings and does not insult or demean them.

Multi-level Thinking - RHD promotes a "win-win" thinking process that encourages the expression of many different viewpoints and rejects one-dimensional thinking.

Empowerment of Groups - At RHD, power resides with the group, not with the individual. Group leaders are empowered to empower others and no person, regardless of position, has permission to treat others in an inappropriate or dictatorial manner.

Decentralization of Authority - Local decision-making should be maximized and, whenever possible, power and responsibility should not be centralized.

Safe and Open Environment - All RHD settings must be open environments where employees and consumers feel safe to communicate their thoughts, feelings, and concerns.

Creativity - All consumers and employees should be actively encouraged and supported to express fresh ideas and approaches, regardless of the degree to which they depart from what is typical or commonplace.

Honesty and Trust - All RHD environments are expected to be places of honest communication that promote and support the belief that each consumer and employee is worthy of trust and must always be treated with respect.

Diversity - Diversity with regard to characteristics such as race, age, gender, ethnicity, culture, levels of education, economic status, religion and sexual orientation are valued and promoted by the organization. The corporation rejects all discriminatory behaviors toward any individual or group.

Organizational Integrity - RHD embraces the obligation to conduct all of its work with strict adherence to the highest ethical standards, including issues relating to laws and regulations and the proper utilization of funds.

Ongoing Growth and Development - The organization is committed to the constant improvement and utilization of its capacity to respond effectively to new social needs and service challenges.

Personal and Professional Enrichment - RHD is committed to creating environments that promote the maximum enrichment of the personal and professional life of each consumer and employee.

Quality Service - All programs are required to deliver quality service.

RHD ORGANIZATIONAL VALUES (FULL VERSION)

RHD is a values-driven organization. It is the commitment to certain values that gives us our particular character, focus and energy. We recognize, however, that these values, no matter how worthy and well intentioned, will not play a meaningful role in organizational life unless all employees strive continually to sustain and foster them. Therefore, we do not merely encourage all members of the organization to support and promote the organizational values; we <u>require</u> that they do so.

Although there are a number of values that are important to the organization, certain values have been particularly relevant to the life of the RHD community and collectively serve as its cornerstone:

- Respect for the dignity and worth of each individual
- Multi-level thinking
- Empowerment of groups
- Decentralization of authority
- Safe and open environment
- Creativity
- Honesty and trust
- Diversity
- Organizational integrity
- Ongoing growth and development
- Personal and professional enrichment
- Quality service

RHD's vitality and strength require that consumers and employees engage in an ongoing dialogue regarding these values at all levels of the organization. The values statement is a living document that is continually open to review and always subject to re-formulation.

Respect for the dignity and worth of each individual consumer and employee - This is RHD's most fundamental value. Each individual has the right to live and/or work in an environment that does not deny or demean his or her fundamental dignity as a human being. Beyond this protection from the negative, destructive behavior of others, each person has the right to expect an active, ongoing affirmation of his or her basic human worth.

Multi-level thinking - RHD promotes an organizational process where the value of creative chaos is openly acknowledged. Such chaos is not seen as formless confusion but as a dynamic tension and ferment that leads to fresh ideas and leaps of creativity. Furthermore, the organization embraces a win/win way of thinking that rejects a narrow "either/or" perspective that divides knowledge into a simplistic calculation of right and wrong or true and false. Instead RHD employs a "both/and" philosophy of knowledge and process that accepts and promotes many different viewpoints. Thus, in instances where two perspectives apparently contradict each other, <u>both</u> can be seen as true depending on the differing experiences and characteristics of the individuals involved. The consequence of this approach is that RHD requires ongoing debate and dialogue and is extremely resistant to one-dimensional thinking.

Empowerment of groups - At RHD, power resides with the group, not with the individual. No individual is empowered alone because all power at RHD, whether it flows from the highest or lowest position in the organization, is <u>shared</u> power. Group leaders are empowered to empower others and no individual, regardless of position, has permission to exercise arbitrary power over another. Furthermore, all consumers, regardless of ability or circumstance, must be empowered by the group or unit to exercise responsible control over their lives to reach their maximum potential. Finally, all employees, regardless of position, must be empowered by the group and its leaders so that they can achieve the maximum development of their capacities.

Decentralization of authority - This value reflects the belief that RHD's work is best accomplished when power and responsibility are dispersed rather than centralized. Consequently, the organizational structure is comprised of many individual units with minimum centralization and bureaucracy. Whenever possible, decisions are made locally including purchasing and the hiring and termination of personnel. This local decision-making facilitates the face-to-face surfacing and resolution of conflict on the part of consumers and employees.

Safe and open environment - Employees and consumers must be able to communicate their thoughts and feelings, their concerns and observations in an atmosphere of trust and mutual respect. They must feel free to advocate for change without fear of retaliation. In an atmosphere which accepts the inevitability of conflict but denies the necessity of hostility, the negating of the value of each person's contribution to the program is resolutely avoided. The criterion for evaluating such contributions is not based on the traditional understanding of success but rather on whether or not conscientious risk-taking, strong commitment, and exceptional effort have been present. Finally, each person's sense of safety is enhanced by the knowledge that all allegations of abuse and demeaning behavior will be immediately investigated and evaluated.

Creativity - The philosophy that underpins this value is the belief that the most effective and satisfying environment is one in which all employees and consumers are actively encouraged and supported to express their beliefs and ideas, regardless of the degree to which these suggestions depart from the norm. Creative working environments continually promote new ideas and approaches. The atmosphere encourages the questioning of authority and avoids the imposition of unnecessary and/or stifling internal regulations. Organizational and unit traditions are appropriately valued but always open to question and debate, while the importance of maximizing choice at all levels of program operations is strongly affirmed.

Honesty and trust - The key to this value is the recognition of the basic goodness and dignity of every human being. Consequently, each consumer and employee begins with the knowledge that he or she is considered to be honest and worthy of trust, although this initial viewpoint may be sharpened and adjusted as a result of time and experience. Finally, every organizational environment is expected to be a nurturing one where each individual is accorded respect and given the consideration of direct and consistent communication, interaction and supervision.

Diversity - RHD recognizes that its consumers and staff represent considerable variety with regard to characteristics such as race, ethnicity, culture, levels of education, economic status, religion and sexual orientation. Such diversity is valued and promoted by the organization while it rejects all discriminatory or negating behaviors towards members of these groups. RHD believes that by celebrating and affirming diversity its organizational life is immeasurably enriched.

Organizational integrity - RHD recognizes its responsibility to conduct all of its work with strict adherence to the highest ethical standards. From the standpoint of legal requirements, all staff and consumers are expected to uphold the laws and regulations pertaining to their organizational activities. With regard to regulatory concerns, each program unit must maintain all appropriate licenses and permits. Integrity regarding fiscal matters requires that each program's financial decisions be based on the greater or common good and not on individual self-interest.

Consequently, all programs are expected to avoid budget deficits, maintain proper fiscal documentation, conduct all financial matters in a timely manner, and manage all funds with proper safeguards. Finally, a commitment to non-discriminatory behavior must characterize all management decisions and interactions.

Ongoing growth and development - Underpinning this value is the understanding that RHD's health and vitality require economic strength and diversity to respond effectively to new social needs and service challenges. With this philosophy, the organization is continually acquiring new technologies, competencies, and resources, which its employees are then able to share with consumers and communities in need.

Personal and professional enrichment - RHD is committed to creating environments that promote the maximum enrichment of the personal and professional life of each consumer and employee. The corporation should be concerned with all areas that impact on life enrichment, including education, health care, housing and leisure time activities. By focusing on these issues, RHD affirms a value that places the growth and development of each member of the RHD community at the heart of its endeavors.

Quality service - All programs are required to deliver quality service. The evaluation of quality involves consideration of a given unit's mission and careful assessments of consumer and customer satisfaction. Long-term program quality requires an environment that promotes a sense of ownership on the part of consumers and staff. This quality is the result of an ongoing process of teamwork and group participation that fosters a feeling of pride and a sense of personal accomplishment.

RHD CORPORATE CULTURE:
A SAFE ENVIRONMENT

RHD believes that employees and consumers alike deserve to live and work in an atmosphere that respects the dignity and worth of each individual.

In order to make this belief a reality, it is necessary to have a safe work environment that encourages the expression of ideas and viewpoints, accepts conflict and the appropriate expression of anger, rejects hostile behaviors, and strives to operate by consensus rather than through centralized authority.

As we expand and articulate our understanding of acceptable and unacceptable behaviors, we continue to improve our work environment and increase the effectiveness of our organization. In the process of thinking, re-thinking, discussing, disagreeing, and eventually reaching consensus, we create our own corporate culture.

CREATIVITY

RHD is committed to providing an emotionally safe environment where employees and consumers can maximize their creativity. New ideas and unconventional ways of thinking require risk-taking. RHD not only accepts but also encourages creative risk-taking in the workplace. Because discussion and implementation of the creativity value may produce disagreement or even conflict between those involved, a conscious effort must be made to create a safe environment for the expression of those ideas.

The expression of diverse views reflects a basic respect for differences. This respect does not necessarily imply agreement but does, however, value the expression of differences.

Everyone has the right to have his/her own viewpoint on any and all topics. When a person's viewpoint is different from or in opposition to ours, it is important that we do not merely discount it. Rejecting another's views by labeling them as "crazy" or "stupid" negates that person's right to think in his/her own way. This behavior is unacceptable in RHD workplaces, and is especially offensive in environments involving children and consumers with mental health issues and/or developmental disabilities.

CONFLICT

A safe environment is necessary in order to foster healthy professional relationships. RHD supports the "Question Authority" premise and values this expression when it occurs between consumers, staff and those in authority. If consumers or staff feel uncomfortable with the instructions or the behavior of other staff or of those in authority, whether at the unit level or Central Office, they have the right as well as the responsibility to challenge this behavior without fear of retaliation or loss of job.

All members of the RHD community need to develop the skills necessary to effectively deal with those who disagree with them. Similarly, it is the responsibility of the leader, or person in "authority," to aid others in expressing their opinions while both work toward resolving the situation. When staff and consumers take on authority, they too act as leaders and assume those responsibilities. Because we all may have the opportunity to take on leadership roles, we all need to be aware of the roles and responsibilities that those positions require. Leaders who are not able to tolerate disagreement or the expression of conflicting views are not in alignment with the corporate values.

EXPRESSING ANGER

Anger or the surge of emotion that comes with strong differences is a normal part of conflict in the work place. Even though we may be upset as strong feelings are expressed, we must avoid being hostile with one another. Those that fear the expression of anger are likely to suppress their feelings and not share their ideas. This in turn slows and reduces the effectiveness of the overall corporation.

RECOGNIZING AND MANAGING HOSTILITY

While conflict and anger are acceptable at RHD, hostility is not.

Hostile behaviors include:

1. Demeaning speech or behavior
2. Negative triangulated messages
3. Threat of abandonment
4. Disconfirming the other person's reality
5. Intimidation/Explosion

Article 2 of this *Bill of Rights and Responsibilities* serves to further clarify RHD's philosophy about and processes for managing conflict and difference within our work community.

DECISIONS BY CONSENSUS

While power is unevenly distributed in RHD and authority relationships do exist throughout the organization, no one is empowered to use his/her authority to insist on personal preferences over those of others. For instance, decisions involving the physical design of the work place, dress codes, staff and client activities, use of discretionary funds and other matters that affect the work environment should include a small or large group process. Although reaching consensus on decisions is time consuming, and the results might be different from the leader's preference, the process itself contributes to an employee's feeling of safety and commitment in the work environment.

RHD places as much importance in the process as in the results. A group commitment to a particular project or idea is of greater significance that the "correctness" of a leader's preference.

SUMMARY

RHD is committed providing a safe work environment where creativity flourishes, conflicts are acceptable, and process is a way of life for all employees and consumers. Our corporate culture is based on each employee accepting responsibility for his/her own behavior, including the responsibility to challenge others when their behavior threatens the safety of the work environment. We all are accountable to each other and our mutual empowerment rests in our ability to maintain a work environment that affirms the individual worth of each employee and consumer.

MANAGING CONFLICT AND
DIFFERENCE WITHIN RHD

The RHD Values explicitly recognize the inevitability of conflict in the workplace, while holding to the position that such conflict need not and, in our corporation, must not involve hostility. The purpose of this article is to supplement the Corporate Values Statement, Article 1 of the RHD *Bill of Rights and Responsibilities* on our Corporate Culture, and the RHD Corporate Policy on Dispute Resolution by describing:

a) Types of hostile behavior which are not acceptable in RHD;
b) Skills that are helpful in constructive, assertive confrontation;
c) Ways to express anger in a non-hostile manner;
d) Mechanisms available to RHD staff members to surface and manage conflict issues; and,
e) Thoughts for "third party" supports engaged to help the parties in conflict situations.

BASIC PRINCIPLES OF CONFLICT MANAGEMENT WITHIN RHD

As written in Article 1, our corporate culture is based on each employee accepting responsibility for his/her own behavior, including the responsibility to challenge others when their behavior threatens the quality of the work and/or the safety of the work environment. We are all accountable to each other. It is our shared responsibility to maintain a work environment that affirms the dignity and worth of each consumer and employee.

Staff at all levels in the organization need to develop and utilize the skills necessary to effectively deal with those who disagree with them. Similarly, it is the responsibility of the leader(s), or the persons in "authority," to assist others in expressing their opinions while all involved work toward resolving a potentially hostile situation. As we all may have the opportunity to take on leadership roles at times, we all need to be aware that leaders within RHD are expected to tolerate disagreement and support the expression of conflicting views in a non-hostile manner.

This corporation has chosen to operate with several basic assumptions. One of those assumptions is that that there are multiple "right" ways or paths we can follow in making decisions, thus there is no one "true" or "absolute" reality. Each person in a situation holds his/her own view of reality, and his/her own perspective about the most effective way to do things. This assumption allows us to recognize that conflict is inevitable and that people will disagree in the workplace. While conflict and difference (or disagreement) are to be expected, explosive or otherwise hostile expressions of anger are not acceptable in RHD.

As a member of the RHD community, it is important to be able to do two things:

a) separate from our own need to be "right" in order to hear and respect others' realities and perspectives; and,

b) differentiate between thoughts (what's going on inside your head) and behaviors (what you do or say).

In RHD, there are five types of hostile behaviors described and named as unacceptable:

1. Demeaning Speech or Behavior

Demeaning speech and behavior involves any verbal or non-verbal behavior that someone experiences as undermining of that person's self-esteem and implies that he/she is less than worthy as a human being. Such behaviors include, but are not limited to name-calling, ridicule, sarcasm, or other actions which "put down" people. Demeaning a person with such physical behaviors as rolling one's eyes when the person speaks or otherwise negating her importance as a member of the community is also unacceptable. Anyone encountering such hostile behavior has the right and the responsibility to surface it as an issue.

2. Negative Triangulated Messages

Triangulated messages involve repeating comments that were supposedly or actually stated by a third party. Usually, but not necessarily, the message carrier keeps the name of the third party secret. Instead of becoming a part of this pattern, one should encourage the messenger to talk directly with the party who initiated the conversation. When third party comments are presented in a group, that group should likewise oppose the acceptance of such triangulated messages.

Specific exceptions to this policy occur when the message or accusation refers to 1) client or staff abuse, 2) theft from the corporation, or 3) threatening the corporate relationship with funding authorities. In such situations, immediate administrative investigation and appropriate action will ensue.

3. Threat of Abandonment

The threat of abandonment in the work environment takes the form of the employer's implied threat of dismissal or the worker's vague threat to leave. While work settings do include the possibility of termination of employment by either party, it is the use of indirect or vague threats, including being ignored or left out of relevant situations, that is sometimes used as a hostile weapon. Threats of firings or resignations create the desire to withdraw from relationships and to reduce creative risk-taking and thus undermine feelings of safety.

If a work relationship is in danger of ending, it is extremely important that communication be clear and open. Supervisors need to be explicit regarding the reasons for possible termination. Employees deserve to know that their jobs are secure unless they are clearly warned to the contrary. Similarly, supervisors need to know if an employee is planning to leave so that strategies can be designed to cause the least amount of disruption to co-workers and consumers.

4. Disconfirming the Other Person's Reality

When one person negates another person's perspective with such statements as, "That never happened," or "Are you out of your mind? How could you think that?" we consider the behavior a means of disconfirming the other's reality. Although one may feel very clear about what he/she experienced in a situation, it is not acceptable to deny that the other person may have had a different experience. It is important to make "room" for the possibility of different realities, at least during the conversation with the other person.

5. Intimidation/Explosion

Hostility is most obvious when it is expressed as yelling, inappropriate language, or physical threats. Such attacks may either stimulate counter attack and possible physical conflict or else withdrawal and submission. Either is clearly destructive to interpersonal safety and is not acceptable at RHD. Even though an employee may have intense personal feelings about a situation, all are expected to control their reactions so as not to endanger the feeling of safety of others. When someone feels and states that s/he is afraid of being attacked, the issue has been raised and both may need assistance to resolve the conflict.

While naming what is unacceptable in this corporate culture is important, giving people tools and options for acceptable behavior is equally important. This document provides some acceptable ways to manage conflict and differences in our workplace.

SKILLS FOR CONSTRUCTIVE, ASSERTIVE CONFRONTATION

■ Clarify your feelings, thoughts, needs and goals in the specific conflict, as well as your own experience and expectations of conflict generally. In particular, identify the conflict behaviors that feel particularly hostile to you.

■ Recognize and respect that the other persons have their own needs and perspectives in the specific conflict, as well as their own experiences and expectations of conflict generally. It is important to remember that different conflict behaviors may feel hostile to others.

■ Directly address the other persons with your concerns or different perspectives.

– Give the other persons a "heads up" that you are going to surface a conflict or difference. This allows them to prepare themselves to respond, not react, to your statements. You might start the conversation with:
  – "I need to express a different view."
  – "Is now a good time to talk about a different view?"
  – "Could we talk about this later/more privately?"

– Use "I" messages to own your feelings and thoughts, allowing the other persons the opportunity to decrease their defensiveness, such as:
  – "I feel hurt when…"
  – "My perspective is…"
  – "I need…"

■ Practice "active" listening. Active listening can be summed up in the statement, "Seek first to understand, then to be understood." The skills of active listening include:

– Face the speaker - show you are listening through your body language.

– Maintain eye contact, to the extent that you both are comfortable.

– Minimize external and internal distractions. Turn off the radio, don't answer the phone, and don't try to take care of other tasks while listening. If your own thoughts about what you want to say next or anything else keep getting in the way, consciously re-focus your attention on the speaker.

– Focus solely on what the speaker is saying.

– Respond appropriately to show that you understand, with such behaviors as nodding.

- Keep an open mind. Try NOT to make assumptions about what the speaker is thinking or intending.
- Wait until the speaker is finished to reply.
- Engage yourself. Ask questions for clarification, and paraphrase what you've heard to make sure that you did not misunderstand.
- Speak only for yourself, rather than bringing others into the conversation.
- Stay with a situation to see it to resolution.
- Engage a helpful, fair third party to assist you and the other person(s) if you do not feel able to go through this process without assistance.

Non-Hostile Expression of Anger

Anger can be described as the primary feeling in a family of feelings which includes fury, outrage, resentment, wrath, exasperation, indignation, animosity, annoyance, irritability, and hostility. Anger, then, is a feeling, not a behavior.

When something happens that seems threaten our sense of safety – whether that threat is to our physical safety or to our self-esteem, such as when we are demeaned – we may experience a rapid rush of feeling angry. The anger rush happens when our emotion hits us before our head can register what we're thinking; the "fight or flight" response is triggered in a flash of a moment. Anger can also emerge a bit slower, when emotion follows from our thoughts or interpretations of a situation.

People often say that they cannot control their anger, and many believe it is unhealthy to do so, even if they could (the "let it all out" concept.) However, while it is true that we do not choose our emotions, we can control to some degree the duration of the feeling and we can control the behaviors we use to express the feeling.

Anger is a pretty seductive emotion – unlike sadness, it can feel energizing and powerful. (It's supposed to – it's the mechanism we have developed to survive!) Indeed, we may need to harness the power of the feeling to get past fears in order to protect ourselves from physical, verbal, or emotional violence or abuse. On the other hand, the longer we allow ourselves to feel the anger, and some of the ways we choose to express the anger, can be damaging both to ourselves and to others. When we linger in the feeling of anger – rolling the thoughts that caused the feeling around in our mind – we may actually increase the intensity of the feeling. And research has shown that venting the anger in an explosion of rage (such as screaming or physical violence) does not eliminate or reduce the anger; outbursts of rage typically pump up the emotional brain's arousal, leaving people feeling more angry, not less. To reduce the duration and intensity of anger, it is far more effective to first cool down, and then, in a more constructive or assertive manner, confront the person or situation directly.

So, how do you cool down when you find yourself caught in the grip of anger? And then, how do you confront the person or situation in a constructive, assertive way?

Defusing Anger and Cooling Down

As stated earlier, the slower form of anger is generated and intensified by the thoughts you have about a situation or interaction. One way of defusing your anger, then, is to seize on and challenge the thoughts that trigger surges of anger. Take a moment or two to figure out what thoughts you are having – particularly those thoughts that stand out most clearly or keep repeating – and try to reframe those thoughts. Ask yourself: Why do I think this? What information do I have to support this thought? What information do I have to dispute this thought? What might the other person be thinking and feeling? If you find yourself unable to look at your thoughts from another perspective, you may want to talk to a more objective third party, asking that person to help you reframe the thoughts.

There are two important points about defusing anger by challenging the thoughts that cause and escalate it. First, the earlier you do it the better, so that your thoughts don't have a lot of time to fan the flames. And second, this manner of defusing anger works well at moderate levels of anger; at high levels of rage it makes no difference because the intense emotion makes it difficult, if not impossible, for you to think straight.

When you cannot think straight, the best thing to do is to cool off physiologically by waiting out the adrenal surge in a setting where there is not likely to be further triggers of rage. There are many ways of cooling off, yet the starting point is to get yourself out of the space in which the situation or interaction is occurring. Just a few options:

- going for a walk or doing other exercise
- watching TV or listening to music (maybe even singing at the top of your lungs!)
- deep breathing and muscle relaxation
- reading and/or writing
- meditating or praying
- anything that distracts you -- one co-worker does laundry!

MECHANISMS FOR MANAGING CONFLICTS WITHIN RHD

It is critical for the parties involved in a conflict situation to **consciously and explicitly** determine the nature of the issues involved, as well as to decide the most appropriate and effective strategies for dealing with those issues.

Once the decision is made to surface the conflict, it is important for individuals to consider the most appropriate course of action. Options include (but are not limited to):

- Direct one-to-one discussion
- Supported one-to-one discussion

Individuals who have a conflict or concern to surface directly with a co-worker or higher level of authority, but who may feel unsafe in doing so alone, may request the presence of a third party. In this scenario, the third party's role is to offer encouragement and support to the person surfacing the conflict, and to ensure that a fair and productive process takes place between the conflicting parties. A third party "support" can be:

- a Citizen Advocate (either from within the unit or from outside the unit);
- other colleague/peer;
- a supervisor or other manager (depending upon the situation);
- a member of the relevant Hub management team;

- a member of the corporate HR Department or the RHD Access Team.

■ Mediated one-to-one discussion

Similar to the option above, however, the role of the third party is to actively facilitate the process that occurs between the conflicting parties so that the parties themselves work constructively toward resolution of the conflict. This role of a third party requires a "neutral" person; the parties in conflict need to view the mediator as someone they trust to facilitate a fair process, and need to understand that the mediator is not a decision-maker regarding the outcome of the conflict. The Citizen Advocates, the RHD Access Team and the HR department are all sources of mediation assistance.

■ Formal dispute resolution/grievance procedure (individual)

Individuals who are in conflict with supervisors about specific employment-related decisions or actions that affect them should be supported and encouraged to utilize the grievance or dispute resolution procedure (as outlined in unit policies and corporate policy). In formal dispute resolution/grievance procedures, the employee raising the grievance is allowed to bring a Citizen Advocate or other peer for support; the employee may choose the Citizen Advocate from his/her own unit or one from the Citizen Advocate group as a whole. As a formal process, the role of the highest level of authority involved in the process is that of a decision-maker or arbitrator; they should facilitate a process for the two parties to communicate with one another, but they retain responsibility for determining the outcome or resolution of the conflict.

■ Facilitated group discussion within work group or unit

When multiple members of a particular unit or work group are in conflict with one another or with supervisors/managers, the group may utilize the support of a third party to facilitate the direct and constructive surfacing and resolution of the conflict. Facilitators may be drawn from members of the unit or work group who are not involved in the conflict, including supervisory or other management staff (depending upon the situation), or from the RHD Access Team.

■ Values Stakeholder Challenge

At times a situation may arise when individuals or groups find themselves differing about the interpretation or implementation of one or more values, or concerned that the values are being compromised with respect to some aspect of a service system. Such a situation may not involve what the individuals perceive as a personal conflict, but instead, the people involved in the situation may have different understandings of what happened, what the others' motivations and/or perceptions were, and what the values mean in relation to the situation. In such a situation, staff may utilize a mechanism named a "Values Stakeholder Challenge." This mechanism is a meeting process that a group of individuals may call when they perceive that a value has been violated or misinterpreted. Again, while interpersonal issues and conflicts are best handled directly and privately, decisions or policies that affect multiple people or groups would be appropriate topics for Values Stakeholder Challenge processes. (Please note: This mechanism should be considered after the parties involved have attempted more direct ways of surfacing and resolving the conflict, as this mechanism may involve additional levels of authority outside of the unit or work group in which the conflict occurred.)

The group calling the meeting identifies as many of the people as feasible who have a "stake" – an interest, concern or responsibility – in the situation and its resolution or outcome, and invites them to join the process. The purpose of a Values Stakeholder Challenge is to surface the issues in the conflict, discuss the issues, and share the different perspectives that the stakeholders have. Each stakeholder's perspective should be respected and validated. Instead of arguing, the stakeholders agree to mutually explore the observations and assumptions on which their points of view are based. It is not necessary that the process lead to a decision on the matter being discussed; however, a decision or change in policy or procedure may come about as the result of new understandings among stakeholders.

Values Stakeholder Challenge meetings can include people from a unit or group plus individuals representing different levels of authority in the corporation, up to and including the Executive Director. It is important to remember that when staff members have decided to reach outside of their unit or work group to call a Values Stakeholder Challenge, they are likely to have developed a level of frustration, fear and/or anger that is not always conducive to constructive conflict management. In addition, the involvement of other levels of authority may contribute to fear, frustration and anger on the part of those being "challenged." Often, the parties involved in the situation have personalized the conflict. In such cases, the emotional levels of the stakeholders need to be recognized and attended to prior to bringing the stakeholders together. For this reason, it is important that all Values Stakeholder Challenge processes be facilitated by experienced group facilitators, available through the RHD Access Team.

■ Formal investigation by higher authorities

Certain issues that are raised by an employee or group in the process of surfacing conflict must be reported to and/or investigated by unit and corporate management. These issues include, but are not limited to abuse or neglect of consumers, harassment of staff (sexual or other), theft, abuse of power/authority, violations of laws or corporate policy, or violation of any of the Employee Rules of Conduct.

Involvement of "Third Party" Mediators & Facilitators in Conflict Situations

If a "third party" – a Citizen Advocate, mediator, or other facilitator – is engaged by the individual(s) seeking to surface a conflict, the first step the "third party" should take is to engage in a fact-finding mission, listening to the concerns expressed from multiple perspectives to better understand the nature of the issues and the course of action desired by the individual(s). In determining that course of action, the "third party" should bear in mind the following principles:

■ Interpersonal conflicts are best handled directly and privately.

Anyone functioning as a "third party" should focus on helping the people in conflict take responsibility for and ownership of their interpersonal conflict situations, and should emphasize the importance of surfacing and dealing directly and respectfully throughout the conflict management process. Carrying negative triangulated messages should be avoided as much as possible.

- Critical to the decision to engage in problem solving is the extent to which the individual wishes to take his or her opponent's goals, interests, desires and personal integrity into consideration. When people perceive their goals to be positively linked, "concern for other" is higher and problem solving more likely than when parties perceive their goals to be independent, or contradictory. The "third party" should gauge the extent to which all parties in the conflict perceive their goals to be shared or positively linked, and base recommendations and interventions on that assessment.

In summary, peer support, mediation, formal grievance, and the Values Stakeholder Challenge are some of the mechanisms available to individuals and groups within the corporation to effectively surface and manage differences. Let's use such mechanisms to sharpen our agreement about how to keep RHD's values alive and working throughout the corporation.

Final Thoughts

Each of us has the right to have feelings, and each of us, in this work environment, has the responsibility to express those feelings in ways that strengthen our self-esteem while maintaining and/or enhancing the sense of safety of others in our workplace.

IMPLEMENTING THE VALUE
OF MULTI-LEVEL THINKING

There once was a group of four blind men who came upon a huge obstacle in the road. The first blind man reached out and felt a large, rough object that was as round and solid as a tree trunk; he told the other men in his party that they had run into a tree. The second man quickly objected; he had reached out and felt a long wrinkled hose waving in the air and so concluded that the object was not a tree, but a hose. The third blind man said, "No, no, no. what we have here is a small, swinging rope with a tassel at the end." And the fourth stated, unequivocally, that the object was none of the things the others had described; instead, he was sure the object was an extremely large boulder. A separate traveler approached the group of blind men and asked, "What are you gentlemen doing with that elephant?"

RHD'S VALUE

"RHD promotes an organizational process where the value of creative chaos is openly acknowledged. Such chaos is not seen as formless confusion but as a dynamic tension and ferment that leads to fresh ideas and leaps of creativity. Furthermore, the organization embraces a win/win way of thinking that rejects a narrow "either/or" perspective that divides knowledge into a simplistic calculation of right and wrong or true and false. Instead RHD employs a "both/and" philosophy of knowledge and process that accepts and promotes many different viewpoints. Thus, in instances where two perspectives apparently contradict each other, both can be seen as true depending on the differing experiences and characteristics of the individuals involved. The consequence of this approach is that RHD requires ongoing debate and dialogue and is extremely resistant to one-dimensional thinking."

"The more perspectives on an issue that a team (group or individual) can consider, the more possibilities exist for effective action. The point is not just to look at one or two extremely different perspectives (i.e.: "either/or," "black/white"), but to capture as many differences of nuance as possible." from The Fifth Discipline Field Book (page 273)

Key Concepts

- appreciate the positive side of chaos, which leads to fresh and creative ideas
- accept and promote many different viewpoints
- accept that people have their own perspectives on reality – one person does not have the whole view
- think "both/and" rather than "either/or"
- increase tolerance for situations that have no clear-cut solutions

Empowering leaders engage staff: they greet new ideas openly and tolerantly; affirm each person's right to have his/her perspective; and, recognize, reward, affirm and incorporate different ideas into their decisions.

What kinds of behaviors promote multi-level thinking?

- actively and consistently affirming when people voice their ideas and concerns
- leading and/or participating in team/group decision-making processes
- offering and participating in job/role-switching opportunities and tours of other sites
- encouraging employees to share training with others in their program and/or the corporation
- asking questions that promote the analysis of issues from as many perspectives as possible
- when there is a disagreement, addressing the other in a respectful, caring way
- encouraging people to try things they've never tried before, or to try things that others say are impossible
- engaging in true dialogue, which does not necessarily result in decisions

- ensuring that groups include people from multiple perspectives
- being aware that silence does not necessarily signify agreement or understanding

What kinds of behaviors interfere with multi-level thinking?

- group leaders stating or indicating that they have answers to issues without engaging others in dialogue
- group members rejecting new views by laughing or putting down a newly offered idea
- group leaders avoiding regularly scheduled group meetings
- group leaders setting the agendas for meetings without input from members
- group members complaining privately about authoritarian decision-making but not raising the issue directly with group leaders
- group members not contributing to group discussions although they have important perspectives to share
- group leaders dominating group discussions and allowing very little time for others to speak

QUESTIONING AUTHORITY

As a key aspect of multi-level thinking, RHD embraces the concept of Questioning Authority. Each of us brings her or his own particular background, information, perspective, job experience, and knowledge of consumers to our jobs. In many cases, an employee's perspective may give him or her access to more or better information or insights than possessed by the person's immediate supervisor or "higher-ups" in the corporation. Each of us has an obligation to bring our expertise to bear on workplace issues.

The value of "questioning authority" does not lie in the rebellious ideal that these words often invoke, but in the principle, inherent in the process of questioning, that understanding and growth arise from challenging the status quo. Imagine, if you can, the condition of our world if Gandhi, Martin Luther King, Nelson Mandela or Thomas Jefferson had not questioned the authority of the systems and thinking of their times. Without inquiry, mistakes, false assumptions, and erroneous ideas remain unchallenged and are perpetuated.

The same is true within the context of the delivery of human services. Because what RHD does is not an exact science, development and improvement of services requires an environment that fosters and supports questions like, "Why are we doing things this way?" or "Isn't there an easier way to accomplish this task?" These questions signify the kind of ongoing analysis that is the key to the maintenance of quality in the services that RHD delivers.

The power to question authority, therefore, is at the heart of RHD's values. However, questioning authority within the context of the workplace is a process that must be balanced against the fact that the workplace exists to accomplish specific tasks and activities. The nature of the relationship of employer and employee is that the employer defines the tasks that are to be accomplished and the broad conditions within which the work must take place. The employee agrees to accomplish the assigned tasks within the established conditions. In the workplace, authority exists to assure that work is completed. This authority cannot legitimately be questioned if the organization is to accomplish its mission.

How the work gets done is quite another matter. Here the issue of authority is by no means fixed.

Authority is defined variously as the power to execute dominating control or influence, expertise, and freedom from doubt. At RHD the first definition is rejected. No one, on any level in this organization, has the power to exercise dominating control. Similarly, as implied in the text above, the nature of the services that RHD provides precludes the possibility that anyone working within this organization can be completely free from doubt. Each person, each situation, has unique characteristics which require continuous adjustment of the parameters of service.

The type of authority that RHD seeks to foster and support is that which arises from expertise. Each aspect of the corporation's operations is populated with individuals who have developed and demonstrated expertise in the area of their professional endeavors. This expertise, born of education, training and personal experience, lends weight to the counsel and advice which these people bring to the workplace. Does this mean that the counsel and advice is not to be questioned? Absolutely not.

Recent research has identified three types of workplace environments, based on the personal and managerial styles of the people who have authority in those settings: Authoritarian, Permissive and Authoritative.

The **"authoritarian"** person thinks obedience, without argument, is a virtue. Authoritarian supervisors and managers tend to set absolute standards of behavior that are not to be questioned or negotiated. They favor forceful discipline and demand prompt obedience. Authoritarian people are also less likely than others to use more gentle methods of persuasion, such as affection, praise and rewards. Consequently, authoritarian people are prone to use more aggressive modes of conflict resolution. Conflicts are dealt with using coercion and intimidation. Workers have little freedom or independence. These workplaces are characterized by a lack of teamwork and much strife as workers attempt to jockey for favored status with the "boss."

"Permissive" people, on the other hand, behave in a kind, gentle way and demand very little. These managers and supervisors place relatively few demands on their workers and are likely to be inconsistent disciplinarians. They are less likely than other people to monitor their workers' behavior. Although the settings in which this management style is used tend to be friendly, workers in them often lack the capacity to work as a team and take little responsibility for their own behavior. Conflicts in this management style are handled in a manner that is often contradictory. Despite the pleasant atmosphere, workers in these environments are often unhappy, expressing the lack of a sense of direction in the enterprise.

"Authoritative" people, in contrast to both authoritarian and permissive people, are neither lenient nor domineering. The authoritative person has rules and exercises personal authority, but rules are explained and reasons are given for decisions. Workers are encouraged to be independent and to express their opinions. Teamwork is encouraged, as is personal initiative and workers in this environment tend to express greater degrees of satisfaction with their work. It is this combination of management strategies that has been found the most facilitative in the development of competence.

In its operations, RHD seeks to establish authoritative workplaces. Questioning of authority is the norm in these workplaces. It is a healthy and dynamic process that is characterized by mutual respect, tolerance for divergent opinions, and openness to the expertise and personal experience of every employee, regardless of their role.

RHD depends upon the creative energies and professional competencies of its employees. By encouraging each employee to "question authority," the corporation maximizes the availability of these vital qualities.

EMPOWERMENT OF GROUPS

At RHD, power resides with the group, not with the individual. Group leaders are empowered to empower others and no person, regardless of position, has permission to treat others in an inappropriate or dictatorial manner.

KEY CONCEPTS

1. Power is to be shared.

When power is shared,

- each person is valued,
- ideas and concepts are limitless and worthwhile,
- the expression of thoughts and beliefs of all is encouraged,
- challenges are problems to solve,
- there is no fear of recrimination,
- no one is isolated, and
- everyone benefits.

2. Decisions are made by the group, not the individual.

When a decision has been made by a group, members of the group have had the opportunity to:

- express their ideas and thoughts,
- present doubts or concerns,
- argue their positions,
- listen to and consider the views of other group members,
- incorporate alterations to the initial plan, and
- question authority.

3. Anyone can develop a group or join a group.

Groups are formed because one or more persons

- feel empowered to do so,
- see a need that should be addressed,
- want to discuss an issue or find a solution,
- believe that "process" is as important as the result, and
- seek a sense of community and camaraderie.

4. Empowerment of consumers is crucial.

When consumers are empowered, they

- have a voice and are heard,
- participate in setting their own guidelines and boundaries,
- are given options which allow them to make decisions for and about themselves,
- feel responsible for their actions, and
- as one consumer said, "[feel] more like being normal."

5. No one person, regardless of position, has permission to exercise arbitrary power over another. All leaders must exercise their power in a manner that respects the dignity and worth of each individual and in a way that is perceived as reasonable by others.

The use of arbitrary power by any person alone over another

- is disempowering,
- is threatening and demoralizing,
- encourages dependence,
- undermines a sense of purpose and responsibility,
- reduces the likelihood of reaching appropriate and effective resolutions when perceived inequities or injustices arise, and
- encourages hostility and distrust.

Note: It is against RHD corporate policy to terminate any employee without the concurrence of at least one other administrative staff member.

Some Behaviors That Foster Empowerment

Empowering Leaders…

- help people believe in themselves;
- are not threatened by the success of others, even of those they supervise;
- encourage others to state their beliefs and respect the principle of questioning authority;
- want to see others receive recognition for their efforts;
- are able to understand each person in the group, including themselves;
- is part of the whole and, in turn, is part of a bigger picture;
- interpret a challenge to their authority as an indication of a safe and open environment; and
- directly ask staff whom they supervise for feedback about their ideas and behavior.

Members of a group express their empowerment when they…

- participate fully in the group by being attentive and offering comments and suggestions;
- discuss a problem situation openly with those involved, instead of gossiping afterwards;
- bring suggestions for solutions to problems and do not expect the leader to provide an answer to every question;
- are respectful when questioning authority; and
- demonstrate willingness to take on related tasks.

Some Behaviors That Interfere With Or Inhibit Empowerment

Inhibiting Leaders…

- ridicule staff or make them feel less of a person for disagreeing with or challenging their decisions;
- do not acknowledge ideas of others;
- do not share decision-making tasks;
- lead through fear and domination;
- confuse empowerment with manipulation;
- may feel threatened by the empowerment of others; and
- may not be able to recall the last time they were challenged about their decisions and decision-making.

DECENTRALIZATION OF AUTHORITY

This value reflects the belief that RHD's work is best accomplished when power and responsibility are dispersed rather than centralized. Consequently, the organizational structure is comprised of many individual units with minimum centralization and bureaucracy. Whenever possible, decisions are made locally, including purchasing and the hiring and termination of personnel. This local decision-making facilitates the face-to-face surfacing and resolution of conflict on the part of consumers and employees.

> "Localness (or decentralization) means moving decisions down the organizational hierarchy; designing business units where, to the greatest degree possible, local decision-makers confront the full range of issues and dilemmas intrinsic in growing and sustaining any business enterprise. Localness means unleashing people's commitment by giving them the freedom to act, to try out their own ideas and be responsible for producing results." —from The Fifth Discipline, pp.287-288

The RHD corporate value of "Decentralization of Authority" is intended to be thoughtfully balanced with the other values, most particularly the values of "Empowerment of Groups," "Multi-level Thinking," "Safe and Open Environment," "Organizational Integrity," and "On-going Growth and Development."

Decentralizing authority means moving power and decision-making responsibility from the Corporate Office to those who are closest to the point of service. In order for this principle to work effectively, people at all levels and in all functions within the corporation need to develop and practice the following skills:

- Sharing power, letting go of need to control;
- Being open to new and different perspectives and ideas;
- Considering how a local decision will affect the corporate system as a whole;
- Facilitating and/or participating in group decision-making processes;
- Listening and responding to others with respect; and,
- Taking responsibility for own thoughts, feelings and behaviors.

What are the principles behind decentralization?

Decentralization of authority, or localizing decision-making, is intended to have the following effects:

- Increased quality of service in meeting "customer" needs—consumers, family, staff, community and funders are better served by the greater responsiveness, flexibility, and creativity that can accompany decentralization.
- Increased sense of "ownership"—staff and consumers at the local level are more supportive and feel greater responsibility and accountability for decisions made with their shared input.
- Increased growth and development, sense of fulfillment, and satisfaction on the part of local staff and/or consumers.

What principles are used to determine what is centralized?

The Corporate Office delegates as many day-to-day operations of systems as possible, and centralizes only those functions necessary to maintain financial responsibility and program integrity.

To meet this goal, the Corporate Office centralizes the signing of contracts, the management of funds, and review and approval of budgets, and is involved in major relationships with government and other contract sources.

Decentralization needs to be honored at all levels in the corporation. Decisions should not be made by individual leaders alone, but with the input of all concerned. Sometimes such process is not possible, but a pattern of authoritarian or autocratic decision-making needs to be questioned, discussed and challenged, if necessary.

Under what conditions will we re-centralize an authority (power/responsibility) that has been decentralized?

RHD does not decentralize power and authority to individual leaders in order that they may create tightly controlled autocratic systems or small "fiefdoms." Power and decision-making are expected to be shared at the local level with the people involved in and affected by that system.

RHD's Corporate Office will intervene in program and/or fiscal operations when there are indications of:

- Misappropriation or poor decisions regarding program funds;
- Decisions and actions that jeopardize a program's licensing and/or funding;
- Local decision-making that reduces options or restricts choices; and/or,
- Leaders making decisions that focus on their own needs and best interests rather than those of their consumers and staff.

The type of intervention used in such situations is determined by the scope and severity of the effect of the autocratic behavior on the people in the system. Before the decision to intervene is made, the dynamics of the specific situation are evaluated and appropriate intervention strategies are carefully considered. Types of intervention include, but are not limited to, investigation, consultation and coaching with leader, facilitated group meetings, conflict resolution processes, temporary or permanent withdrawal of specific decision-making powers, and probation or termination of leader.

The Corporate Office prefers that each unit operates with as much autonomy as possible while continuing to use the Corporate Office services and implementing the RHD corporate values. When a unit chooses to function in isolation without regard to the values, the Corporate Office may find it necessary to re-centralize authority.

IMPLEMENTING THE RHD VALUE OF DIVERSITY

"RHD recognizes that its consumers and staff represent considerable variety with regard to characteristics such as race, ethnicity, culture, levels of education, economic status, religion, developmental ability and sexual orientation. Such diversity is valued and promoted by the organization while it rejects all discriminatory or negating behaviors towards members of these groups. RHD believes that by celebrating and affirming diversity, its organizational life is immeasurably enriched."

Diversity is the strength of Resources for Human Development, Inc. The foundation of the corporation is built on the diversity of the people whom it serves and of the staff who provide the services. Diversity of race, religion, culture, educational backgrounds, abilities and outlooks adds a richness and depth to the corporation that needs to be encouraged and embraced. There is no place for prejudice in this corporation. Moving beyond known, or even unknown, prejudices will open a new world and improve one's quality of life.

The goal of the corporation is not to make everyone alike and conform to one way of thinking and living; it is not to put all of us together to become alike in a melting pot. Instead, we strive to acknowledge and appreciate the uniqueness in each of us and to embrace those differences in all of us. Our goal is to create an environment in which each individual is able to bring his or her "whole person" to work, while not demeaning or negating others. To do so, we need to balance "assimilation" with holding on to the positive, enriching quality of our differences. We differentiate between accepting and respecting our differences and imposing one preference over another.

We acknowledge that leaders (individuals and groups) within our organization often make and implement decisions and that, as human beings, their decisions are based on situational factors and their own perceptions and biases. However, we believe that there are no absolute "right" decisions in any situation, which means that there may be numerous "good" decisions in a given situation. We expect our leaders to draw from multiple and diverse perspectives and to then use their best judgement when making decisions that affect others.

"HOWS" - ACCEPTING, CELEBRATING AND PROMOTING OUR DIVERSITY

Develop Self-Awareness

The first step in creating a work environment in which all members are enabled to bring "who they are" is for each of us to become more self-aware. We need to explore how the messages sent to us through our racial, religious, ethnic, socio-economic, and family backgrounds have influenced our current cultural assumptions and biases. We should take time to reflect on the aspects and qualities of ourselves we most value, and why. In this way we are building a greater sense of self-esteem – finding what we love and value in ourselves – so that we will be better able to find what we can love and value in others, even those individuals and groups that seem so different from us.

We do not want to act as though we each do not have biases; instead, we want our awareness of those assumptions and biases to serve as "red flags" which will help us to consciously avoid behaving toward others in ways that are based on those biases or that feel negating or demeaning to others. For this reason, it is important to create opportunities and environments in which people in a workplace can surface and talk about biases and assumptions – to make "undiscussables" more discussable so that we learn together how our differences can enrich the decisions we make and the actions we take.

Affirm and Celebrate Our Differences

Programs and groups throughout the corporation must demonstrate their commitment to the affirmation and celebration of diversity. We should also create a variety of mechanisms to address the programmatic impact of having different races, genders, lifestyles, and communication norms in the workplace. This commitment can be promoted through such actions as participating in culturally-sensitive orientation and training, organizing multi-cultural events, involving all members in the process for selecting program holidays, and holding brown bag lunch discussions on issues relating to diversity.

"HOWS" -- REJECTING DISCRIMINATORY AND/OR NEGATING BEHAVIORS

Recruitment, hiring and other employment practices should reflect the corporation's commitment to having a multicultural workforce.

Beyond the legal requirements contained in our corporate policies, RHD is committed to creating employment opportunities for people from diverse backgrounds in order to enrich the decisions and work of the organization. We must ensure that no individual is rejected for employment based on the fact or perception that the individual is a member of any specific group. If an individual has a need that is based on inclusion in a particular group (religious, sexual orientation, disability, etc.), the individual has both the right and the responsibility to join with others in problem-solving when his/her need conflicts with the needs of the program.

As one way of helping us remain conscious of our diversity goals, all programs and groups throughout the organization are requested to periodically look at the composition of the membership in their group, and to reflect on the reasons for and impacts of that composition. Based on such reflection, the group may want to make decisions about how it will move forward in creating and valuing a diverse membership.

Systems must be in place throughout the corporation and the programs to vigorously investigate and resolve allegations of discriminatory practices and negating behaviors.

Any employee who feels that he or she has been unfairly treated or has concerns about discriminatory or negating behavior in the workplace is strongly encouraged to bring the issue(s) to the attention of his/her immediate supervisor, a Citizen Advocate, Unit Director, Hub point person or RHD's Human Resources Director. Complaints will be investigated, and anyone found to be engaging in discriminatory or negating behaviors will be subject to disciplinary action, up to and including termination.

Often, however, bias and discrimination are demonstrated in very subtle ways, such as excluding a certain person from group activities because he is different from the other members (for example, he may be the only male, the youngest or oldest, more or less educated, of a different race or religion or sexual orientation, etc.). The more subtle the discriminatory or negating behavior, the more difficult it is to challenge. As with other hostile behaviors, it is important to remember that at RHD, hostility is "in the eye of the beholder," that is, it is defined by the receiver. In the example given here, if the person feels demeaned or negated by being excluded from group activities, he has the right to raise his concerns, regardless of what the others in the group intended by their behavior.

Finally, one of the reasons people do not challenge discriminatory or negating behaviors in the workplace, especially the more subtle behaviors, is the fear of retaliation. As with discrimination, retaliation can be overt or subtle; regardless, retaliation is not acceptable at RHD. Any employee who feels that he or she has been retaliated against for surfacing and challenging discriminatory or negating behaviors is encouraged to bring the issue(s) to the supervisor, Unit Director, Hub point person or RHD's Human Resources Director.

Summary

Bias, discrimination, negating behaviors, retaliation...none of these actions are acceptable at RHD. Our goal is to recognize and eradicate even the subtlest of discriminating behaviors.

Diversity can be, and in this corporation, is powerful; it demonstrates our strength, freedom, joy, learning and quality. When we create an environment in which each person's uniqueness is valued, honored and appreciated, we have the opportunity to bring out the best in each of us. And this, in turn, enriches the life of the organization.

IMPLEMENTING THE VALUE
OF "QUALITY SERVICE" WITHIN RHD

"Quality Service—All programs are expected to deliver quality service. The evaluation of quality involves consideration of a given unit's mission and careful assessments of consumer and customer satisfaction. Long-term program quality requires an environment which promotes a sense of ownership on the part of consumers and staff. This quality is the result of an ongoing process of teamwork and group participation which fosters a feeling of pride and a sense of personal accomplishment."

What is quality service? Can we define it?

In RHD, we see quality in the visible and often measurable development and changes in our consumers and our staff. We also perceive that "quality" means doing our best to achieve the goals of our program/team. It often means providing what is needed, even if what is needed is not being explicitly asked for.

Quality service and creativity go hand in hand. It requires each of us to bring our creativity to the work we do in order to continually discover new ways of helping consumers reach their maximum potential, and of exceeding our customers' needs and expectations. Quality service is never "completed" or achieved once and for all, nor is it a constant state; the challenge is to acknowledge when we are moving toward what has already been defined as quality service for a consumer or customer, and when we need to stop and redefine quality service based on the current information and situation.

Quality service involves "going the extra mile" because we really care about the people we serve, we care about our own personal satisfaction and the level of **pride** we feel about the work we do, and, in many cases, we care about the connection between our work and our spirituality – serving a higher power or a god of one's own understanding.

"Going the extra mile" may look like being a helper or mentor to new staff, even though that responsibility may not be outlined in your job description, so that everyone on the team is moving in the same, positive direction. It may look like spending a little extra time and energy to read between the lines and find the true meaning behind the words or actions of a consumer or staff member so that the individual feels heard and responded to. It may look like pausing for a moment to be fully "present" in a relationship with a co-worker or customer, genuinely responding to a greeting rather than simply replying "hello, fine" without thinking about how, in fact, you **really** are or how that person **really** is that day.

Quality service occurs when a group works together in a mutually supportive relationship to:

- provide maximum freedom of choice for the consumer or customer
- provide support for minimizing choices that are deemed "harmful" to the individual consumer or others
- demonstrate patience with the development of the consumer
- demonstrate commitment to the consumer
- demonstrate empathy with one another and treat each other with respect

In a sense, "quality service" means that we are continually "raising the bar," in terms of what we expect and how we respond, for each other. The story below is shared as an example of what we mean by "quality" in everyday work life:

During a team meeting of the staff in a residential unit, one direct care staff person raised the topic of the way the team had been serving the meals of a consumer who, for medical reasons, had to have his food pureed. The staff person voiced her observation that staff was putting all of this gentleman's food into a blender together and serving it as a "shake" of sorts, and she shared her opinion that the consumer deserved to have his food presented in a way that made it a real "meal" that he could share with his housemates. She talked about how important she thought it was that he feels like an equal member of that household. She asked for concurrence from her team mates that this consumer should be served his meals at the table with his housemates, with his different food items (although pureed) presented attractively in separate sections of his plate. Her point was that, although blending the food together and serving it all at once was easier and more efficient for staff and met the consumer's nutritional needs, that method did not treat him like a dignified human being for whom eating a meal in his home with his housemates was a right. The staff team responded to her by agreeing that her suggested way of serving meals to this particular gentleman would be implemented.

Where does quality service come from?

The source of quality service needs to be separated from educational degrees or formal authority/power, because at the most fundamental level, the quality of any service is affected by the staff's **relationships** with the consumers and with one another. These relationships, when of a high quality, are characterized by a sense of kinship with the consumer, as well as a sense of ownership and empowerment that is shared by both the staff and the consumer. Quality service does not come from the "head" alone; having a degree does not guarantee quality service. The relationship characterized by "joining" and by "kinship" is generated and supported in large part by the "heart."

A Group Process

The true measure of quality is demonstrated in the **process** of delivering the service, not solely in quantitative measures and outcomes. Perceptions of the quality of a service need to be elicited from all "stakeholders" – those people affected by the service, as well as those with relevant information, authority and resources to affect the service. All stakeholders should be encouraged to express their opinions about the service as well as their satisfaction with the service. Indeed, the essence of quality service is a willingness to continually search with other stakeholders for better ways of achieving "satisfaction" and "quality."

When delivering quality service by involving multiple "stakeholders" in the process, we can expect at least some conflict or difference of opinion regarding what constitutes "satisfaction." It is common for us to be committed to providing quality service, yet we often prefer to avoid conflict, especially in groups. RHD appreciates that verbalizing difference is often experienced as painful or frightening. However, we cannot seek quality in an open way if any one of us expects to be attacked. For this reason, the implementation of this value is intricately connected with that of the other values, especially "Safe and Open Environment," "Respect for the Dignity and Worth of Each Individual," and "Diversity."

The level of **pride** that members of a group feel about their work is a critical facet of the process of creating and delivering "quality service." Staff satisfaction and pride fosters continual improvements in the quality of services provided by that staff, which in turn bolsters the group's sense of satisfaction and pride. It is not an "either/or" situation—**to genuinely provide quality service, the corporation and each program must be attuned to and supportive of continually increasing staff satisfaction and pride in the work that staff groups do together.**

Summary

In summary, the creation and delivery of "quality service" in RHD involves finding a healthy combination of two key measures: the degree to which stakeholders are encouraged to have their own voice and choices, and the degree to which differences among stakeholders are managed constructively and respectfully. At the most fundamental level, however, is the concept that true "Quality Service" comes from the heart and spirit of individuals working together in healthy relationships, with a sense of ownership of and pride in both the results and the process of their work.

TRIANGULATED NEGATIVE MESSAGES

Resources for Human Development is consciously working to create a safe and creative environment for all of its employees. Toward that end, we have developed this corporate "*Bill of Rights and Responsibilities*." As part of this effort, we formally reject behavior in the workplace that we find to be hostile and threatening to others. The passing on of **Triangulated Negative Messages** is one of those behaviors that we want to stop wherever possible. Below is a definition of Triangulated Negative Messages, as well as some of the impacts and intervention points related to them. As one way of stopping these behaviors, you will note that we encourage employees to reveal who is carrying negative messages about others; "shining a light" on the negative message carrier will help discourage such behavior at RHD, and we will all benefit in a safer work environment.

Definition of Triangulated Negative Messages (TNM's)

A triangulated negative message is a communication process in which one person (the "carrier") conveys a negative message from another person (the "originator") to a third person (the"receiver"). The content of the message is:

- feelings or thoughts the originator has expressed about the third person,
- often conveyed to the receiver as "a secret", and
- usually unsolicited by the receiver

Diagram:

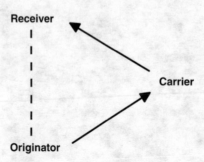

Results of Triangulated Negative Messages

The results of this type of communication process are numerous, including, but not limited to, the following:

Receiver of the message:
- increased anxiety and concern
- decreased sense of safety and trust
- disempowerment by being asked to "keep it a secret" when he/she needs to surface and deal with the conflict

Carrier of the message:
- inner conflict and anxiety about being responsible for conveying (and the potential results of conveying) the message
- increased control over the tone, feeling and content of the original message

Originator of the message:
- reduced control over the tone, feeling of the message intended
- possible reduced responsibility for the content of the message since it was conveyed by someone else
- possible reduced trust in the individual who acted as a carrier

Impact of Triangulated Negative Messages on the Work Environment

TNMs often result in an atmosphere that feels unsafe for all members of an organization – those involved in the situation, as well as those observing the process and results of the situation. By allowing conflicts to be managed through the use of Triangulated Negative Messages, conflicts are often forced "underground."

Underground conflict is indicated by high levels of stress, loss of productivity, competition, perceived helplessness, chronic complaining, and/or sabotage. Also, people may "leave by staying"; if quitting isn't a realistic choice, a person with deep-seated, unresolved conflicts may physically remain in the situation but his or her spirit, energy, enthusiasm, etc. will leave and passive-aggressive behavior may result.

Dealing with Triangulated Negative Messages

Regardless of the role you are playing in a TNM situation, the first thing to do is to take a good look at your own behavior and motivations.

In an organization, we all have a part in creating the current reality, no matter what our position. In a relationship, we both create the outcome. In a team, what we do or don't do is a part of the process and the results.

Accept your responsibility for creating both the current reality as well as the potential reality, and choose to create a healthier and more productive potential reality.

THEN: If you have a negative emotion/thought about or conflict with someone, consciously choose what you will do with it.

If it is a true conflict, deal directly with the person with whom you have the conflict – don't give away the power of or responsibility for your feelings to another who is outside of the conflict.

If it is an emotion or thought that you simply need to "vent" to someone, choose your confidante and be clear with her/him that you are "venting" and that you do not want the message carried outside of your conversation.

If you are engaged by someone who has a negative message about a third party, consciously choose what role you will play.

If you perceive that there is a conflict between the originator of the message and the third party, choose to be a **"supporter"** of direct surfacing and resolution of the conflict. Be clear with the originator that you will not carry the message <u>for</u> him/her, but that you will be there, emotionally and/or physically, for him/her as the conflict is surfaced and managed.

If you perceive (or hear directly) that the originator simply needs to "vent," choose to be a **"listener."** Do not take it upon yourself to carry the message forward. A word of caution – take care of yourself by setting limits regarding the amount of "venting" to which you will listen. If a particular originator is using a great deal of your time and energy (whatever you feel is "too much"), be clear with him/her about the point at which you need to stop listening. At that point, suggest that the person either deal directly with the conflict (and you choose to become a "supporter" instead), accept the reality as it is, or find another listener.

If you choose to be a "carrier" of the negative message, understand that you have no right to confidentiality or invisibility. By choosing to convey the message, you are giving up your right to stay out of the conflict situation; in fact, you have chosen to become a player in it.

If you receive a negative message about yourself from a carrier, consciously choose how you will react.

If you feel that the TNM indicates a conflict between yourself and the originator (or you feel hurt or unsafe as a result of the TNM), check out the reality of the message with the originator. Surface the issues and feelings, and problem-solve in order to manage the conflict.

Remember, once a carrier has conveyed a TNM, you should not feel any responsibility to keep quiet about the source of your information about the conflict. Understand that you have both the right and the power to deal with information that impacts you, and your sense of confidence and safety in the workplace.

If you feel anxious or afraid, engage a "supporter" or a "listener" in your organization to help you face the conflict in a healthy way. Do not expect or ask anyone to convey your feelings or reactions for you; otherwise, you are choosing to be a TNM originator yourself, and a very unhealthy cycle will continue.

OPEN COMMUNICATION

Open communication – simply put – means two things in RHD:

- ANYONE (or any group) can speak with ANYONE ELSE within the entire corporation directly about ANYTHING at all at ANYTIME; and,
- NO ONE is permitted to use his/her "authority" to prohibit the open and free communication of ideas or concerns any employee may wish to express.

In RHD, as in all other work environments, there are defined lines of authority. Each of us has a "boss." In most companies all communication of ideas and/or issues is required to flow up this "chain of authority" to some higher place at which decisions are or are not made. Such communication frequently gets blocked, lost or changed somewhere along the chain, often by a supervisor who is either indifferent or fearful. Consequently, many workers choose to stifle creative ideas rather than risk the disapproval of their supervisors. They may speak "unofficially" to other co-workers about their concerns, suggestions and ideas, but they may be hesitant to express themselves to their "boss". In some cases, the employee has spoken directly to a supervisor and his/her ideas have been rejected or dismissed. They can see no positive results. If the person thinks there is no place else to go – no alternative – then discontent and/or apathy emerge and, too often, great ideas are lost.

We decided long ago that we did not want such a rigid structure regarding human communication to exist officially at RHD. Our written Values Statement speaks about the "open environment" we promote. That means that when the ordinary "chain of authority" avenue is felt to be ineffective by an employee – for whatever reasons – that employee is welcome to choose another avenue of communication. He or she may speak respectfully with anyone at any level within the corporation and expect some response/resolution to the issues presented in a reasonable time frame. We recognize that it is important for the continued health of our organization that the ideas and concerns of all staff are heard and considered.

Obviously, it is recommended that an employee first approach his/her immediate supervisor with concerns or suggestions since that is the place where most issues can and should be rapidly addressed. However, on those occasions when that approach is not sufficient or comfortable, all employees are encouraged to identify another person or persons with whom they can share their insights and who will follow through with appropriate actions.

In summary, NO ONE in RHD is empowered to PROHIBIT open communication between members within our corporate community.

CREATIVITY

"This 'telephone' has too many shortcomings to be seriously considered as a means of communication. The device is inherently of no value to us."

–Western Union internal memo, 1876.

Resources for Human Development is committed to supporting and encouraging the formulation and expression of new concepts and is willing to take a nontraditional level of risk in order to implement good ideas. Creativity is one of the core values upon which RHD was built. In 1976 a woman named Portia Sperr approached Bob Fishman with the "out of the box" idea of starting a museum where children could touch and interact with the exhibits. No already established museum was willing to incorporate the idea into its mission. With the help of RHD, this idea became a reality and the *Please Touch Museum* was born.

This groundbreaking idea has since been copied throughout the country. Almost any museum that you walk into today has at least one interactive exhibit for their visitors. In fact, these are generally the most popular exhibits. What if RHD had taken the same stand as everyone else and squelched an idea that was perceived as a risk?

"So we went to Atari and said, 'Hey, we've got this amazing thing, even built with some of your parts, and what do you think about funding us? Or we'll give it to you. We just want to do it. Pay our salary, we'll come work for you.' And they said, 'No.' So then we went to Hewlett-Packard, and they said, 'Hey, we don't need you. You haven't got through college yet.'" *-Apple Computer Inc. founder Steve Jobs on attempts to get Atari and Hewlett-Packard interested in his and Steve Wozniak's personal computer.*

How do I know if I am, or could be, creative?

Every living, breathing human being has the potential to be creative. Each of us is a unique individual capable of creating. We are, quite simply, a creative species.

Most of the obstacles to creativity can be found within you:
- Fear of criticism.
- Lack of confidence in oneself.
- A narrow definition of what creativity is, ie. creativity means much more than just being good at arts and crafts.

What can I do to increase my creativity?

Creativity requires patience and a willingness to work for a creative outcome rather than simply waiting for enlightenment. The first step to becoming more creative is giving yourself **permission** to do things creatively. The second is overcoming your **personal blocks** to creativity. It really helps to think of creativity as a skill or set of skills. By practicing, one can get better at using them. So whenever you have a chance try to do mundane things in novel ways—it will make them more entertaining and you will get used to expressing your abilities.

What do I need to do before presenting my idea?

Before presenting new ideas, whether at a site, unit, or corporate level, ask yourself the following questions:
- Does this idea benefit those around me and/or society in general?
- Do we have the funds or resources to try it, and, if not, can I figure out how to get the funds or resources to try it?
- Do I have the energy and commitment to pursue the idea?
- Am I willing to take a personal risk in implementing this idea?
- Is it legal?

If you can, with good faith, answer "yes" to these questions then no one should tell you that you cannot attempt to implement your idea. EVERYONE has the right to implement her or his ideas.

Implementation, of course, does not guarantee success, but unless you try you will never know if your idea could have succeeded. You must not let others discourage you from your vision.

"The concept is interesting and well-formed, but in order to earn better than a 'C', the idea must be feasible." –*A Yale University management professor in response to Fred Smith's paper proposing reliable overnight delivery service.* (Smith later founded Federal Express Corp.)

What are the responsibilities of the person with the idea?

"If I had thought about it, I wouldn't have done the experiment. The literature was full of examples that said you can't do this." – *Spencer Silver on the work that led to the unique adhesives for 3-M "Post-It" Notepads.*

- You must believe in your own idea and passionately follow through with trying to get it heard.
- Don't let one "no" stop you. If you feel that your idea meets the above criteria and you do not get a positive response from the first person you approach, find someone who will listen. Places you might try are your HUB team, the Accentuate the Positive Committee, the Citizen Advocates.
- Find a way to attract a network and to build on your idea. When you express your idea you may be surprised to find that others have a similar idea or can connect you with additional resources to support your idea.
- Own your idea and be willing to do the hard work of making your dream become a reality.

What are the responsibilities of the person listening to the idea?

"Drill for oil? You mean drill into the ground to try and find oil? You're crazy." –*Drillers who Edwin L. Drake tried to enlist in his project to drill for oil in 1859.*

- Increase your availability and willingness to listen to new ideas. Commit to being responsive when someone presents an idea to you.
- Empower and encourage the person with the idea by asking questions and giving constructive feedback.
- Assist the individual in carrying out his/her idea, to the best of your ability, **without** taking ownership away from that individual.

- Look at your own fears or reservations when presented with a new idea. Are your reservations rational? As the listener you are being asked to take a leap of faith.
- Decrease times when you, unwittingly, squelch or discourage someone's idea.

What are everyone's responsibilities?

"Everything that can be invented has been invented." – *Charles H. Duell, Commissioner, U.S. Office of Patents, 1899.*

- "Stir the waters". Encourage discussion of new ideas and ways of doing things.
- Find ways to help get new ideas heard.
- Demonstrate respect for individual viewpoints and ideas.
- Be willing to own your idea while opening yourself up to collaborating with others.

Summary

All ideas do not have to be earth shattering, monumental ideas. Small changes can mean huge changes in the lives of others. Examples of ideas that have meant a great deal to RHD and others are:

- the 2nd Floor News (Ridge's newsletter where staff and residents express their ideas and emotions);
- the mural in the back staircase of RHD's Central Office;
- Tigerman (a superhero who promotes anti-violence with our youth);
- the Community Gardens of Chester County (a garden for low-income residents that encourages self-reliance, good nutrition, and recreation);
- Endow-A-Home (a program which enables low-income women with children to purchase their own homes);
- Citizen Advocates (a way for "line staff" to have a voice within the corporation); and,
- Capital-To-People (a for-profit program within RHD that supports employee-owned businesses that create wealth in low-income areas).

While most people at RHD have heard of and recognize these initiatives, there are ideas that are being born every single day that change peoples' lives for the better. Examples of small ideas that make a **BIG** difference are:

- finding a new recreational activity for an individual who's become bored with his or her routine;
- buying a microwave oven to increase someone's independence;
- developing a booklet of information about the services that RHD employees can access for support within the organization; and,
- encouraging a staff member to pursue further education.

As part of the RHD family we are all encouraged to utilize unconventional thinking. Ideas need to come from ALL LEVELS of the corporation in order for RHD to continue to flourish and preserve its diversity. We must not be afraid to express our ideas and to support others in having their ideas be heard. Unless your idea has been heard and tried, nobody has the right to tell you "It can't be done."